What people are saying about

21st Century Fairy

An interesting, well documented survey of beliefs about the fairies, from long ago up to today. Includes references to folklore and modern storytelling, as well as personal experience. A great foundation for folks to build their own understanding of the Good Folks on.

Catherine Kane, author of *Adventures in Palmistry* and *The Practical Empath*

This is a wonderful new offering from Morgan Daimler, whose extensive research and knowledge of fairy lore has been a real boon to the Pagan community and beyond. Looking at the evolution of fairy, how they can be perceived and encountered in the modern world, exploring outdated perceptions as well as finding what remains constant are discussed in this book. There are other issues which are unique to this work and which are not represented broadly, such as racism in fairy media and the ongoing representation devolved from Victorian perspectives. For all those interested in fairy literature and lore, this book is a real asset as well as being great reference material.

Joanna van der Hoeven, author of *The Path of the Hedge Witch* and *The Hedge Druid's Craft*

T0019919

Pagan Portals
21st Century Fairy

The Good Folk in the new millennium

Pagan Portals

21st Century Fairy

The Good Folk in the new millennium

Morgan Daimler

MOON
BOOKS

Winchester, UK
Washington, USA

JOHN HUNT PUBLISHING

First published by Moon Books, 2023
Moon Books is an imprint of John Hunt Publishing Ltd., No. 3 East Street, Alresford
Hampshire SO24 9EE, UK
office@jhpbooks.net
www.johnhuntpublishing.com
www.moon-books.net

For distributor details and how to order please visit the 'Ordering' section on our website.

Text copyright: Morgan Daimler 2022

ISBN: 978 1 80341 046 3
978 1 80341 047 0 (ebook)
Library of Congress Control Number: 2022931809

All rights reserved. Except for brief quotations in critical articles or reviews, no part of this
book may be reproduced in any manner without prior written permission from the publishers.

The rights of Morgan Daimler as author have been asserted in accordance with the Copyright,
Designs and Patents Act 1988.

A CIP catalogue record for this book is available from the British Library.

Design: Matthew Greenfield

UK: Printed and bound by CPI Group (UK) Ltd, Croydon, CR0 4YY
Printed in North America by CPI GPS partners

We operate a distinctive and ethical publishing philosophy in
all areas of our business, from our global network of authors to
production and worldwide distribution.

Contents

Other Fairy Titles by Morgan Daimler

Aos Sidhe
Meeting the Irish Fair Folk
978-1-78904-937-4 (Paperback)
978-1-78904-938-1 (ebook)

A New Dictionary of Fairies
A 21st Century Exploration of Celtic and Related
Western European Fairies
978-1-78904-036-4 (paperback)
978-1-78904-037-1 (ebook)

Fairies
A Guide to the Celtic Fair Folk
978-1-78279-650-3 (paperback)
978-1-78279-696-1 (ebook)

Fairycraft
Following the Path of Fairy Witchcraft
978-1-78535-051-1 (paperback)
978-1-78535-052-8 (ebook)

Fairy Queens
Meeting the Queens of the Otherworld
978-1-78535-833-3 (paperback)
978-1-78535-842-5 (ebook)

Fairy Witchcraft
A Neopagan's Guide to the Celtic Fairy Faith
978-1-78279-343-4 (paperback)
978-1-78279-344-1 (ebook)

Living Fairy
Fairy Witchcraft and Star Worship
978-1-78904-539-0 (paperback)
978-1-78904-540-6 (ebook)

Travelling the Fairy Path
Experiencing the myth, magic, and mysticism of Fairy Witchcraft
978-1-78535-752-7 (paperback)
978-1-78535-753-4 (ebook)

This book is dedicated to my children.
Beannachatí na Daoine Maith daoibh go bragh.

Author's Note

This book is the result of many years of conversations with friends as well as seeing a widespread idea that fairies are somehow primitive or archaic, despite the many modern anecdotes and stories we have that show them in modern settings and contexts. I eventually taught a workshop on modern fairies and subsequently was asked if I had a book on the subject. Since I didn't, I decided to write one, which, honestly, is my solution to a lot of things. This text weaves together material from workshops I've taught, blogs I've written, and many conversations I've had over the years to create what hopefully will be a useful resource for people seeking to understand fairy and fairies in a modern context.

Every book ultimately reflects the biases of the author and for me these are beings that I believe exist in some sense and context and have been believed in by humans across millennia. This view undoubtedly colours my opinions but I have done my best to be objective in what is shared here, at least as much as I can be. I want everyone, no matter what your viewpoints are, to find some value in this book.

I personally favour using APA citation in my writing and so throughout this book when a source is being cited you will see the name of the author and date of the book in parenthesis after that. Each chapter will also have end notes expanding on points that don't fit neatly into the larger text but are important to touch on. I hope this approach will help create a good resource for readers, whether you are here out of curiosity or because you are seeking a deeper understanding of this subject.

Introduction

For many people the idea of belief in fairies as real beings that can be interacted with is a relic of the past, something to be found in dusty books and old stories. But for others the Good Folk continue to be a strong and clear presence in our thoroughly modern world, still seen and still encountered in many places, both by people seeking them and those who never thought of them at all. But when the subject of fairies comes up what many people imagine is shaped by mass media which is fond of depicting fairies as either primitive creatures – animalistic or clad in bark and leaves – or as anachronistic beings who appear as if through the mists of time, in medieval knight's armour or gowns. Yet when we stop and study encounters and anecdotes from the late 20th century and 21st century a different picture emerges, one of a hugely diverse array of beings, some indeed clad in medieval wear but others in jeans and sneakers, some who are merged with the natural world and others who are thoroughly urban. The world of Fairy and its inhabitants then isn't – you'll forgive the analogy – some bug trapped in amber but a living, vibrant reality that encompasses everything humans can imagine and more.

This book is meant to be something of a very loose guide for seekers of Fairy to find this vibrant world, moving through the anachronisms and tropes to the living heart of Fairy where it intersects with the human world today. It looks at the ways that understandings of fairies have changed over the last hundred years, how they are integrated into the 21st century, folkloric material that is still as strong today as ever, and offers some advice for seekers to move forward balancing belief and scepticism in a healthy way. It is also a blend of my own thoughts and experiences with other sources, mostly academic books. I know it may be a bit jarring for some readers to move between a more academic view of something and my own personal thoughts on it but I feel like both aspects are important and my own spiritual practice and belief system is built on this hybrid model. I study this as a subject of interest but I also have my own personal experiences with it and both sides of my interactions will be included here.

I believe it's important to note up front that there is a very long and probably endless debate about whether humans have ever or can ever see fairies as they truly are or whether every fairy experience across history has been shaped by human perception. If we can see them as they are, under exceptional circumstances, through their allowing it, or through innate ability, then looking across the range of historical and modern accounts we can draw some definitive conclusions about the subject. However, if we cannot – if every encounter anyone has ever had is merely a reflection of either the human's expectations or of layers of fairy glamour[1] – then anything and everything we have to say on the subject is only reflecting human belief[2] across time periods. Either way I think it's useful to look at these depictions, how they've changed, and to anchor these beings firmly in our very modern world. But going in to this book it's important to be clear that this is not a simple topic and that there are different perspectives on even the most basic aspect of whether or not we can perceive these beings in any kind of truth.

It also has to be mentioned, of course, that anything and everything with fairies is always contradictory and difficult to entirely define, so that while we will be focusing here on the modern iterations and interpretations of fairies the reader shouldn't take this to mean that the other, older forms of fairies don't exist as well in the modern world. For every story of a human encountering a thoroughly modern fairy in jeans and a t-shirt there are others of someone seeing a bark-clad sprite or fairy knight in ancient armour. It is best to remember that Fairy and its inhabitants are, in the most crucial ways, outside of the human concept of time. I might also remind readers of what I refer to as the first rule of Fairy: nothing is certain.

We tend to be so caught up in the ideas of fairies wearing leaves or in Renaissance Faire attire because these are the images that we get from mass media, whether that's popular novels or movies. There has been a slow movement away from this recently, perhaps as urban fantasy[3] has gained popularity and the idea of powerful, human-like fairies in the modern world has found its way onto television through shows such as Lost Girl and Carnival Row[4]. But reshaping popular perception of fairies is a slow process and the 20th century ideas are still lingering and effecting people's expectations. For anyone seeking to understand fairies in the 21st century I strongly suggest looking at how the media has shaped your views and making an effort to put any preconceived notions you have aside and embrace the idea of a much more complex, complicated reality.

Moving forward into the rest of this book here's a thing to think about – it's very easy to get wedged into our own point of view. I constantly try to check myself on this because it's something that sneaks in slowly and hardens so that we aren't even aware of it. When we talk about Fairy and the beings within it, you'll see a lot of very diverse and often antithetical views and opinions out in the world and also in this book.

Here's the thing... They may all be true. The catch is that none of them are the only truth, any more than a human who lives in a city describing their home and lived experience can be said to be describing 'the human world and life' in toto. Because we all know that humans and the human world are diverse, and one description doesn't – can't – define all of us and the same is true with fairies not only cross-culturally but in general.

Someone can live their whole life seeing and dealing with tiny little garden sprites, and to them that may be what Fairy and fairies are. And by their experience they are accurate. But that isn't all of it, even if it is a small true portion, just as someone who has only ever seen and experienced glowing balls of light or human-sized wingless beings is not seeing the entirety of who and what fairies are.

Do you see what I'm saying here? Someone can be completely honest in their view and their view can be true, by that measure, but that doesn't mean that view is all there is. Living in a rural area doesn't erase the existence of cities, coming from a Western culture doesn't negate the existence of every other culture – and there's always more to Fairy than any of the pieces we see and understand. Keep an open mind, on all sides.

Chapter 1

Do Fairies Evolve?

A key question to begin with, and one that I have been asked more than once, is do fairies evolve? This question is less about whether fairies as a category of beings show signs of what humans would call evolution in a species and more about whether they are capable of change and adaptation to the human world they interact with. I think the answer to this is a definitive yes, as we can see by looking across a range of things related to fairies which have changed, sometimes radically, in the last hundred years. And let's be honest this is drastic change in a short time but it is also very much in line with how drastically human culture has changed across the 20ᵗʰ century and into the 21ˢᵗ. In this chapter then I want to look at several aspects of how we envision fairies that are considered or assumed to be universal now but are actually relatively new in the wider scheme of things, as well as a couple things relating to fairies that we do have evidence have changed over recent years.

Tiny Fairies

Let's look at the example of fairies perceived as tiny beings which is so pervasive across not only popular culture but also modern fairy encounters. I want to start with a bit of a deep dive into this because I think it beautifully illustrates the way that a concept about fairies can begin in the fringes and slowly but surely grow in the popular imagination until it comes to dominate the subject. After this section I'll move on to several other similar ways that fairies have changed across belief into what is now the most common understandings of them, but I hope that this first section will show in general how this process works.

So for many people today the word fairy immediately invokes

images of a tiny winged being – and we'll get to the wings in a bit – but why do we envision fairies as tiny?

The fairies of folklore – historic and modern – are depicted across a wide range of sizes and forms, from about 18 inches tall to well over 13 feet. These beings are known as shapeshifters and their size is often fluid and changeable, or at least human perception of their size isn't constant. Also specific types of beings are known to have particular sizes and appearances, such as the selkies who are human-like on land and seals in the water. In many Irish fairy encounters the beings are described as more or less human sized, a feature we see as well in Scotland. Some specific beings like Leprechauns were known to be about 18 inches to 3 feet tall, depending on the story. As with so many aspects of folklore this subject isn't clear cut or easy to simplify but includes a spectrum of possibilities. However, we can say in a very general sense that the idea of tiny, insect sized or smaller fairies isn't common across Western European folklore, yet it has become ubiquitous in the popular imagination. Let's take a look at where this idea comes from.

Where we do find tiny fairies is in England, particularly English literature but with possible roots in older folk beliefs. Katherine Briggs discusses several medieval English examples of what she terms 'diminutive fairies' which are described as about as tall as a finger is long; these were either specific types of beings or specific individuals in context, rather than all fairies more generally. The earliest such account comes from Gervase of Tilbury in the 13th century who describes beings he calls 'Portunes' which are between a half inch and a foot tall[5] (Briggs, 1976). While a foot tall is on the smaller end of fairy sizes within folklore in general it isn't as tiny as we will find later as fairies are refined into the early modern period literature.

The earliest description I have found in writing of tiny fairies comes from Shakespeare's Romeo & Juliet, completed in 1597, where he describes the fairy queen Mab as *'In shape no bigger*

6

than an agate stone; On the forefinger of an alderman' (Shakespeare, 1980). Mab is not only as tiny as the stone in a finger-ring but is said to travel in a wagon fashioned from insect parts: wheels spoked with spider legs and a wagon cover made of grasshopper wings. This idea is expanded several decades later in Michael Drayton's, 1627, 'Nymphidia' a poem which describes the English fairy court. In this poem the fairies are firmly established as tiny beings who can fit into flowers and use small natural objects for their construction – spider legs to build walls and bats wings to cover their roofs, for example. This comes to us from English literature (the literate class as opposed to direct folk belief) and is an idea we will see repeated in later works as well, blending the idea of diminutive fairies with Paracelsus's elemental divisions of these beings to create the tiny air and earth fairies that would later take hold in popular imagination. As to why fairies were so far reduced, as Diane Purkiss so aptly says it:

The Elizabethans and even more so the Jacobeans loved the miniature. In their hands, fairies shrank to tininess. ... Reducing the other to miniature scale reduces it to manageability too, making it laughable. (Purkiss, 2000, pp. 181 & 182).

Despite this diminishment, the fairies of this period were still seen as having power and influence, particularly over human dreams, madness, and crops.

The Victorian era is one of the most pivotal points in how popular culture today would come to view fairies, with a surge in interest in romanticized folklore, nature, and entertainment. The fairies of folk belief became subjects of retellings and fairies more generally were rewritten and redefined away from dangerous and powerful beings and into the fodder of children's stories and art. These fairies were firmly rooted as well in the miniaturization that had begun with Shakespeare and persisted through English literature and poetry, finding expression in

Pope's 1712 'Rape of the Lock' for example, where fairies are definitively small and generally powerless as well as in William Blake's late 18th and early 19th century works which described tiny fairies. Victorian era literature, though, took these existing ideas and framed them for children, reducing fairies not only in size by favouring the insect comparisons but also infantilizing and moralizing them. As Carole Silver explains it:

> As the elfin peoples became staples of children's literature, the perception grew that they themselves were childish.... Some of the tales promoted a false set of conventions, one that made, the fairies tiny and harmless – moral guides for children or charming little pets – and a tradition of sentimentalization and idealization developed. (Silver, 1999, p187).

Being tiny was then directly connected to both being childlike and being powerless, creating a being that was physically miniature and more decorative than dangerous.

Into the 20th century this idea was further refined in popular culture with Cicely Mary Barker's flower fairies and with JM Barrie's 'Peter Pan' taking to the stage. While fairies in art during the Victorian period were often shown as small both of these sources were popular and gained wider traction in the popular imagination and refined fairies down to their essential tweeness. Barker's fairy art featured tiny childlike fairies connected to and often clothed with specific flowers and plants. Her fairies then were small enough that flower petals could form a skirt for one and an acorn the perfectly sized cap for another. Barrie's 'Tinkerbell' in print was both feminine and seductive but on stage transformed into an indistinct ball of light who communicated through the sound of bells, existing largely through Peter Pan's perception and translation (Kruse, 2019). The tiny, glowing, nature-bound fairy may well be understood as the conglomeration of all of these influences into the 20th century.

So, while tiny fairies can be found in older material, particularly in England, they represented only a small portion of the wider range of fairies. Artwork such as sir Joseph Noel Paton's 'The Quarrel of Oberon and Titania' displays this range of sizes and appearances, including both human sized beings as well as tiny ones, rather than the exclusively tiny sized fairies that some modern sources depict. It is also important to understand that tiny fairies are largely coming from English literary traditions rather than folk belief, a point that Silver notes in her book and which I have traced out here. The tiny fairies that are seen and experienced today and which can be found in modern fairylore exist parallel to older folk beliefs, often contradicting them, and represent one unique strand of belief rather than the entirety. You will find as we move forward that this is often true of aspects of fairies that people believe to be universal.

Wings

Moving on from tiny fairies let's look at where the idea that fairies have wings comes from since this is one of the other main changes in fairies across the last several hundred years.

Whereas tiny fairies can be traced back to English literature, winged fairies have a very different root: the theatre. Wings served as a quick device to show an audience that an actor/actress was a fairy. We can see examples of this usage from the 18th century onwards. From there it entered the public consciousness and became especially popular in Victorian artwork, and has become ubiquitous today for many people.

Prior to this we do not see fairies in artwork with wings, nor do we hear them described in stories as having wings; when they fly in folklore it is through the use of magic, often by turning an object into a horse that can move through the air or simply by what we might call levitation. Shapeshifting is another main method fairies in folklore use to fly. Wingless fairies are still the mainstay in folklore; however, anecdotal accounts are increasingly involving winged fairies as the idea is so firmly embedded in the popular imagination now.

The concept itself likely grew out of the depiction of angels and devils in artwork, as well as human souls, that showed them winged. This would have naturally lent itself to the need for a visual aid to help an audience identify a character as Otherworldly. And while angels had bird wings and demons had bat wings fairies took on insect like wings, paralleling the wider associations growing between fairies and insects across this period (and touched on a bit in the above section).

Pointed Ears[6]

It's generally assumed in Western culture today that elves, and more widely many types of fairies, have pointed ears and the image has become so ingrained in popular culture as to be a trope. Yet why do we picture elves and fairies with pointed ears, when most descriptions from European[7] folklore emphasize how human-like these beings appear?

When we look at descriptions of fairies, under different names, from folklore we generally find their human-like appearance being emphasized. In the 'Ballad of Thomas the Rhymer' Thomas initially mistakes the Fairy Queen for the Virgin Mary; in the 'Ballad of Tam Lin' Janet has to ask Tam Lin to clarify whether he is truly a fairy or was once human, making it clear there's no obvious physical indicators of his nature (Acland, 2017). As Andrew Lang says:

There seems little in the characteristics of these fairies of romance to distinguish them from human beings, except their supernatural knowledge and power. (Wimberly, 1965).

Yeats, in the late 19th century, relates this description of a Fairy woman given to him by a woman in Ulster:

She was like a woman about thirty, brown-haired and round in the
face. She was like Miss Betty, your grandmother's sister, and Betty
was like none of the rest, not like your grandmother, nor any of
them. She was round and fresh in the face... (Yeats, 1902).

In all of these examples and others across folklore we see fairy
people being described without pointed ears and notably with a
very human-like appearance, usually the only indication of their
Otherworldly nature comes through their actions, demeanour,
an energy or feeling around them, or a perception people have
of them as such. This has held true in many modern accounts
as well, although as we've touched on already the popculture
images do have a powerful influence as well.

So where then do we get the idea that elves and fairies have
pointed ears? The answer is a bit convoluted and requires
looking to the way that Christianity depicted demons, the way
that Greeks described satyrs, and finally Victorian art.

The concept of elves and fairies with pointed ears in Western
culture is likely rooted in Christian demonic imagery. This is because
Christianity in seeking to explain the existence of elves and fairies
fit them into the cosmology as a type of demon or fallen angel,
which logically led to people imagining demonic characteristics
onto fairies. As far back as 1320 we can find depictions of demons
with pointed ears, usually along with other physical deformities,
especially animalistic features (Bovey, 2006). These pointed ears and
horrific appearances are in sharp contrast to the way that angelic
and divine beings are depicted, emphasizing through physical
depiction the hellish nature of these demonic beings. Whereas the
saved souls and angels are emphatically human, the demons are
just as emphatically inhuman with their obvious animal features,
including their ears. This way the animalistic demons are more
frightening while the human-like angels are appealing. In folklore
we also often see fairies described with animal features, including
tails or webbed feet, as well as physical deformities like hollow

backs; although fairies are just as often described as beautiful as they are grotesque it's likely this tendency towards animal features made it easy to merge the two groups. Because Christianity chose to depict demons in the way that it did and because they explained fairies in their cosmology as a type of demon or fallen angel, and because fairylore itself described fairies as having physical features that could fit the later Christian descriptions of demons, there was a certain inevitability in the artistic depictions of the two types of beings blending together.

Although it may be understandable as to why Christianity chose to show demons as horrific in artwork, pointed ears included, this does beg the question of why Christianity chose to depict its demons this way when in the Bible they are described as fallen angels, and angels are certainly not horrifically animal-like in appearance. Although some angels can look disturbing based on how they are described in the Bible – cherubim, for example, have four wings that are covered in eyes – most are simply referred to as 'men' without any further detail, implying that while they were not human, they also weren't exceptionally strange looking (KJV, 2017). In fact, in stories where they show up, some people may recognize them for what they are but others often do not, which we see in the story of Lot and his angelic visitors in Genesis 19; this at least implies that they can pass as human. The Bible also makes it clear that Satan and his servants – read demons – masquerade as angels and servants of light which would seem to contradict the idea of demons having a grotesque appearance (KJV, 2017).

Looking further back, though, we see that there were some beings in Greek and Roman mythology that did have animalistic features and potentially pointed ears, including beings like satyrs. Satyrs were described with ears that could be either donkey like or goat like in shape, and in artwork this is easily perceived as pointed (Atsma, 2017). In the King James version of the Bible there are references to satyrs[8], which may be a mistranslation of the Hebrew word for a type of spirit (Jackson, 2017). Even though a mistranslation is likely in that case it speaks to a cultural perception that related satyrs to demons, likely reflecting cultural tensions of the time. It is likely then that the classical depictions of satyrs influenced that later Christian depictions of demons.

Early depictions of elves and fairies in artwork show them in line with folklore depictions, that is mostly human-like in appearance although they may be either beautiful or ugly and were sometimes shown as very small. As we enter into the Victorian era, we begin to see elves and fairies shown with pointed ears, probably based on popular imagery of Puck, which in turn drew on demonic imagery that was drawing on the depictions of satyrs (Wright, 2009). Puck was a popular folkloric figure that had long blended fairylore and demonology, understood as a type of fairy, individual being, and also a name for the Devil (Wright, 2009). This blurring of fairylore and Christian cosmology was fertile ground for artwork and laid the foundation for a wider understanding of fairies through this lens; the artists of the Victorian era slowly refined the concept so that what began as pointed ears only on the wildest of fairy beings eventually spread to pointed ears even on the delicate winged nature sprites. By the 19th century artists began depicting elves and fairies with pointed ears almost exclusively. By the 20th century we see these descriptions entering written media with both prose and poetry describing elves and fairies with pointed ears. Even Tolkien tentatively described his Hobbits with slightly pointed ears and his Elves, at one time[9] with pointed or leaf shaped ears (Dunkerson, 2017). The concept has now become ubiquitous, spreading throughout popculture and into folklore, so that it is simply taken as a given that elves and fairies have pointed ears. More recently I have noticed a shift particularly in anime and RPGs[10] from the smaller leaf-shaped ears of Victorian art and Tolkien to excessively exaggerated, elongated ears that stretch above or beyond the head and are more reminiscent of donkey ears in shape, ironically returning to the older satyr-style. Pointed ears became a quick way to signal to a viewer that the subject of a piece wasn't human even if they seemed so in all other ways, or in other cases to emphasize their inhuman nature. Once this was adopted as a visual cue and then into fiction it slowly worked its way into anecdotal experiences, until we find the idea of pointed ears widespread in fiction and fairylore.

To summarize this section then, we have traced the way that the modern image of the fairy as tiny, winged, and with pointed ears has come together, particularly across the last hundred years, to form the most popular image of fairies today. Some readers may not think this matters but I really believe that to understand how fairies evolve in human perception we have to understand that the image we have of them today is fairly new and understand how it came to be what it is. This also raises the question of whether people today who see or perceive fairies as tiny, winged, and with pointed ears are seeing what they expect to see, if human belief has shaped these beings in any way, or if that particular type of fairy represents but one iteration among many.

Moving forward from looking at physical aspects of fairies that have changed I want to take a quick look at a couple secondary aspects of fairies that we can also find evidence have adapted to the passing of time and to the change in human cultures. I think this is another thing that is important to consider in understanding the ways that fairies may evolve across time.

Clothes

I've mentioned a few times now that many people expect fairies to wear either vegetation or some archaic dress and I believe this is because of the strong influence of art and mass media, which I've already discussed. In many anecdotal accounts fairies appear to people wearing clothing that blends in reasonably

the biscotti offered as a free sample in front of a cafe. And we'll forget that all of these are the exact same delicious trap.

When we look at folklore it's very clear that eating the food of Fairy is dangerous. The most well-known prohibition around food and fairies is certainly the rule not to eat fairy food. The general belief is that to eat the food of fairies is to be irreversibly bound to them and their world. We see a wide range of anecdotes centred on this idea, usually featuring a human who has encountered a group of fairies and been invited or inveigled to join them, been offered food or drink, and is then cautioned by a human among the group (often recognized as a recently deceased community member) not to take the offered meal. The warning always includes the explicit message that if the food or drink is accepted the person will not be able to leave and return to the mortal world or their family. In the ballad of 'Childe Rowland' the protagonist is advised to *"bite no bit and drink no drop"* when he goes to Fairy to rescue his sister if he wants to succeed and return again to Earth with her. There are some exceptions to this, particularly in situations when the food is being offered by one of the monarchy of the Otherworld, but overall this is one of the most consistent prohibitions we find. It binds a person to the place, either through obligation or transmutation. But when we think of what food we'd be offered what do we imagine? Probably not donuts and milkshakes.

I can understand why people tend to have a set idea of what food they'd be offered in Fairy. In the folklore it's often simply called food and that's not helpful. When it is specified, in the 'Adventures of Connla' or the 'Ballad of Thomas the Rhymer', we see apples being mentioned. Not for any Christian symbolism in my opinion, at least not originally, but for older mythic themes of youth and immortality. Apples and the Otherworld have very old connections after all, to the point that Manannán's realm there is named 'region of apple-trees' [Emain Abhlac]. In Rosetti's poem 'The Goblin Market', the fairy food was fruit of various kinds. It's easy to go with the idea of fruit, and because we have an ingrained view of Fairyland as primitive and existing in our past people tend to naturally picture historic dishes or simple foods. And in fairness you may encounter or hear stories of people being offered that sort of thing; In Cutchin's book 'Trojan Feast' he mentions modern encounters where people were offered berries, pancakes, and milk to name a few. So that does still happen and I don't want to imply it doesn't.

But just as there are cities to be found in Fairy and modern encounters of fairy beings that look very much like humans but are not,[11] we may also encounter or be offered fairy food that is not what we expect. Personally I find baked goods to be pretty common, especially sweet breads, rather like bread-shaped cakes, and little cakes. I think though that if they were trying to lure a person in, they would offer whatever seemed most alluring and innocuous to that person. If you happen to run into a group of the Good People who are trying to trap you, they may offer you the prerequisite apple, but they may also offer you chocolate chip cookies just like you loved as a child or invite you to sit down to pizza, which just happens to be your favorite. There was a post on Tumblr that mentioned the Good People using a coffee shop to trap the unwary, where you were fine if you stuck to what you paid for but you were doomed if you accepted anything offered for free – because in Fairy nothing is ever free.

This aspect of fairy evolution is just as crucial as any of the others because it shows the ways that the fairies are very much present in the modern world.

Having said all of that I hope that readers have a good idea at this point of a few of the ways that fairies have changed and adapted across the last century and are comfortable with the idea that these beliefs are fluid and changeable in line with human society.

Chapter 2

Fairies in the Modern World

Now let's switch gears a bit and look at some aspects of fairies in the modern world. Specifically I want to discuss the presence of fairies in cities, fairies and modern technology, and the crossover between fairies and UFOs/aliens. I realize that second one may seem like an odd topic to be getting into here but it's a complicated subject and something that I am often asked about so I think it's worth covering here.

Urban Fairies

Articles on fairies often, consciously or unconsciously, tend to focus on fairies and fairy encounters in wild or rural settings but this is only part of the picture. Across the breadth of the material – past and present – we see a wide range of Otherworldly beings including those that are found in human habitations and cities.

While it's true that some fairies do avoid humans or prefer to live in more desolate areas, many of the Good Folk are inextricably intertwined in human lives. I think it's important to understand this and to avoid an overly narrow view or understanding of these beings, so I'd like to talk a bit about why we tend to exclude cities from our understandings of fairies, the folklore that can tie them to cities, modern anecdotes, and examples of cities in Fairy itself. Hopefully this will give people some food for thought on the subject.

First off, I think we need to talk about a common misperception: that you can't find fairies in cities or that they wouldn't want to be there. This seems to be rooted in the common idea that fairies are entirely or only nature spirits, which is itself a misunderstanding of the taxonomy of fairies. Even if we accept that viewpoint, however, that should not limit the presence of fairies in human cities. Cities still have plants, trees, insects, wildlife, and even pockets of natural spaces in which one might find nature spirits or land spirits if one believed those were the sum total of fairies. As much as we may sometimes prefer to see cities in contrast to rural or wild spaces the truth is that cities are merely adapted from those spaces and still hold a bit of wildness and nature within them. The energy is different, of course, but it is still there. When you get down to it all of the world is natural and so nature spirits can and will exist everywhere.

Another argument hinges on the idea that fairies are averse to iron and human cities have a lot of that. It is true that modern cities tend to be built with a lot of steel and iron and that many types of fairies are warded off by this material. However, not all fairies are sensitive to iron and even those who are may not avoid a place where iron has been used for building if the iron is covered by other materials.

In folklore, for iron to be effective as a deterrent or protection it often (not always) has to be bare; for example, in Sikes 'British Goblins' there is a story of a man in Wales who is being harassed by fairies as he travels and they only flee when he pulls his dagger. The dagger in the sheath wasn't enough to ward them off, but the bared metal was. There is another story of fairies who would visit a man working in a kitchen, without seeming to be bothered by the iron cutlery or cookware, but would flee if a knife was held in their direction. From this we can, hopefully, see that the presence of iron building material by itself wouldn't keep fairies out of a city.

There is folklore of fairies to be found in cities, castles, and other human places. In Sussex, for example, a goblin was said to guard treasure in a hall at Herstmonceux (Fairy Folklore, 2020). There are also fairies like the Abbey Lubbers and Buttery Spirits which lurk in the food storage areas of abbeys, inns, taverns, or generally dishonest households, stealing the value from the food if the humans are greedy or fail to protect it with proper blessings (Briggs, 1976). And, of course, the famous MacLeod fairy flag was by some accounts given to the family by a fairy woman in the MacLeod's castle. Fairies are also well-known across folklore for enjoying human fairs and races, both places with a lot of humans and human activity. All of these are examples of fairies that are or were associated with places with larger human populations or activity and demonstrate that fairy folk are not put off by human activity or settled areas.

One of the most intense personal experiences I have had happened in a city of 27,000 people. It was around four in the morning and I saw a white fairy hound crossing an empty field; it disappeared about 2/3rds of the way across moving towards me. My other experience with fairy hounds – or at least black dogs – happened in a slightly larger city (40,000 people) when a friend and I saw two black fairy dogs. As with my sighting of the white hound the two black dogs disappeared afterwards, were unaccompanied, and were moving directly towards us. In the case of the two dogs they also seemed to respond to things we were saying (we hoped they wouldn't cross the street and they immediately did) and somehow crossed in front of us without being seen, which should have been impossible. In both instances I was in the middle of a human city with the usual city activity although I will note that during the second experience there was a notable lack of human presence around.

Beyond my own personal experiences other people have also encountered fairies in modern cities. A great resource for such modern encounters, of all varieties, is the 2018 'Fairy Census' which is available free online and which has gathered an array of anecdotal accounts including some from cities. For an example, from that source, #8 is a woman in Birmingham England in the 1990's who described seeing a 6-foot tall elf lying across a tree branch in a city park (Young, 2018, page 29-30). In the same source, account #10 also takes place in a city, this time inside a store. These modern encounters are in the same spirit as older ones and continue a long tradition of people having personal experiences of fairies in various ways and places, including cities. There is a tendency to view fairies as limited to the realm of gardens and wilderness but I urge people to rethink this. We have abundant evidence both in the older material and in modern accounts of fairies in human cities and of cities existing in the world of Fairy. We need to be willing to consider the entirety of the evidence and to take it for what it is rather than try to overlay our own opinions and biases onto it. The idea that fairies would only be found in wilderness, in my opinion, reflects a romanticism of those beings that lessens who and what they are rather than adding to our understanding of them.

Technology

The subject of fairies and modern technology is an intriguing one, and one that encourages some good discussion and debate, often predicated on the individual's personal understanding of what fairies are. I'd like to dig into some ideas around this concept here, with the understanding that I'm speaking from my own view of fairies as diverse groupings of beings within folk belief that have always interacted with humans, can be human-seeming, and can interact tangibly with the human world. Obviously other people's opinions may vary, but I think to really anchor fairies in the 21st century we have to take on this subject as well.

While there is often a tendency to view fairies, et al., through a heavily anachronistic lens we do have some precedent for the idea of these beings interacting with or interfering with human technology. A quick look across folklore shows us that fairies have a long history of using or borrowing human tech, contemporary to the time periods of the stories. For example, Briggs, in her various works, discusses the motif of fairy borrowing, including references to stories where fairies would borrow hand mills, a type of small hand-held grinder, which was the cutting edge technology of the time. At the least this demonstrates that the Good Folk have had an interest in new human tech, an ability to adapt to it, and desire to acquire it. Another pertinent example here are Gremlins. Gremlins – not the movie sort – are a type of fairy being that we initially see appearing in the First World War reported by military pilots and mechanics. They would damage planes and other human machines, cause general havoc, and all sorts of mechanical problems. If you are familiar with the old Twilight zone episode 'Nightmare at 20,000 Feet' where the plane passenger sees the gremlin trying to sabotage the engine mid-flight, that encapsulates the folklore reasonably well.

There is certainly an idea shared among many people I've talked with that 'tech fairies' are a thing, perhaps as a kind of ultra-modern ghost-in-the-machine type gremlin. This is a term that is applied to the sort of random tech weirdness people experience that can't be easily explained and so is personified; since it is along the lines of fairy mischief, both harmless and malicious, that we find across stories this personification is labelled 'fairy'. My own experience with this ranges from tech inexplicably failing right before I could post things discussing deeper personal gnosis around fairies to an auto-fill on my phone that seems to be possessed by some sort of spirit. Are these modern aspects of fairies or something else? I don't know but it is definitely interesting to contemplate and fits in with our discussion here.

A more important and possibly insidious – although, of course, theoretical – aspect of this discussion is the idea of enchantment via technology, that is that the Good Folk are intentionally using human technology to influence people. This is rooted in the very old idea of fairies using glamour or magical enchantment to deceive and influence human perceptions, to lead humans into specific actions, or lure humans to a specific purpose. The idea of glamour is then combined with technology, particularly social media and videos, giving us the possibility of casting magic through the medium of media.

The idea of fairies in technology and fairies using technology are nascent ideas as far as I know within the wider concept of fairylore. Yet as humans move forward and become more and more technology driven, I believe that we will see an increase in stories and discussions of fairies, in various guises, associated with human innovations. As much as I advocate for a clear understanding of the difference between folklore and fiction, I do think this is one area where urban fantasy can help us broaden our minds away from the rigid expectation that fairies must be primitive and even technophobic. Listening to modern anecdotal accounts from people who have experienced these beings is also very useful and shows a small but important pattern of stories that mention fairies in modern dress, in modern cities, and using or familiar with things like cell phones, computers, and cars.

As we established in the first chapter, the fair folk have always evolved as humanity has evolved and so it is only logical that they would incorporate human tech into that as well, at least in some way.

Fairies and Aliens

To begin, nothing I am going to say here is groundbreakingly original. But this is a topic that comes up from time to time, that I have been asked about many times, and I want to address my own opinions on it as within the community of people who believe in the Good Neighbours there tend to be a couple schools of thought. Suffice to say that the people who hold the opposite opinion to mine use the exact same evidence but argue the other angle so I am in no way trying to say that my thoughts here are the truth in an objective sense. But I do think that it's an aspect of modern fairies worth considering.

Here's my personal opinion on whether there is any connection between fairies and extra-terrestrials, given as a personal opinion (so no reams of citations).

I believe that modern stories of aliens and alien abductions are actually fairies and fairy abductions re-framed to fit within

20th and 21st century human expectations. Fairies have been a part of belief and folklore as long as we have written stories from the various cultures we find them in[12]. However, as we have moved, culturally, into the modern and post-modern period, fairies have largely become relegated to children's stories and nostalgia, at least in popular culture. This left a contextual void for people having experiences to use to explain what they were experiencing. This void was filled by fiction and film as popular culture embraced the idea of extra-terrestrials and our cultural consciousness became saturated by these new stories.

The first aliens appear in fiction in the late 19th century and in Hollywood in the silent films of the early 20th century; the idea, however, really bloomed post World War II in both speculative fiction and film. The first UFO sighting in the US is thought to have occurred in 1947; the first reported abduction in 1961. This timeline is important to contextualizing the subject of fairies and aliens as it roughly overlays the same timeframe that fairies were being moved in popular culture away from powerful folkloric beings and into the realm of small, less powerful (or powerless) beings.

When we compare fairylore and alien and UFO lore we see some striking similarities:

1. Fairies are well known for stealing humans of various ages, who they may or may not return later. Stories of alien abductions also feature humans being taken away for varying periods of time.

2. In both fairy abductions and alien abductions people may return with physical marks or scars

3. Some types of fairies are known to take humans by lifting them up through the air; modern UFO encounters sometimes also feature such occurrences.

4. The reason for taking people, including forced reproduction, are also consistent between both fairy stories and alien

abductions although how the two play out historically versus currently vary.

5. Time is noted to move differently in Fairy, usually with a human experiencing a short amount of time in Fairy only to find that a long amount of time has passed on Earth. In the same way alien abductions and UFO encounters often note a distortion of time.

6. Fairy encounters with beings like the Mâran include a person awakening to a feeling of terror and sleep paralysis. Some alien abductions involve a person waking unable to move and paralyzed.

7. Food can play a role in both fairy encounters and alien encounters. In traditional fairy encounters fairies would often offer food to people, usually with the intent of trapping the person in Fairy so that they could not leave. In some alien encounters the person is offered food of various sorts as well although the intention is unclear. In fairylore when the food was refused there are stories of the fairies trying to force the person to eat the food or drink the liquid, or physically punishing them for refusing; in the same way in some alien abduction stories there have been accounts of people forced to eat or drink substances, in some cases violently.

8. Fairies were noted to dance in circles and to leave behind fairy rings in their wake. These could be rings of mushrooms or of darker or lighter grass. UFOs have also been noted to leave circular marks in places they have been seen landing, sometimes flattened grass sometimes burned areas.

9. Similarly, the idea of strange lights being attributed to fairies has a long history in folklore, often associated with danger, while UFOs are described as both lights in the sky as well as strange lights seen through trees. These sites afterwards, of both types, are noted to have strange properties and effects on people.

Appearance is an issue that is also brought up but given that fairylore tells us that the Good People can use glamour to appear, however, they want – and to make our surroundings appear to us, however, they want – I find this particular angle the weakest. If we expect them to look like what science fiction has taught us aliens will look like, I have no doubt that is exactly what we see during an abduction experience.

There are people who will say that we see far fewer fairy encounters today and fewer fairy abductions, yet now we have this phenomena of alien encounters and abductions, which have many of the same hallmarks. To my mind it seems that the fairies are no less active but have simply switched how people are perceiving their activity so that those who believe in or are open to believing in aliens get aliens, while those who believe in fairies continue to have experiences more in line with older folklore. Fairies used to be feared and that fear had power; aliens still are feared as an unknown and technologically superior factor.

So, short answer, I think alien encounters and abductions are just fairies dressed up in modern guise. Which is a pretty effective method of both misdirection and control, if you happen to be Them.

For further on this subject I suggest reading 'Passport to Magonia' and 'Trojan Feast' both of which discuss fairies and aliens as an interwoven subject.

Whatever your own opinion about fairies and aliens – and it is a contentious subject – there is undoubtedly evidence connecting fairies to human cities and to human technology. Fairies exist in the modern world and they are not exempt from its influence anymore, perhaps, than humans are.

Chapter 3

Modern Fairyland

Just as with the subjects we've already covered, the fairies themselves, people seem prone to describing and viewing Fairy through a primitive lens. When people talk about their experiences they are usually couched in terms of wilderness and wild places or occasionally of settings that may be described as historic, such as castles or cottages. And that is not to say that these places can't be found in Fairy just as we can find these places in our own world, because they certainly do exist both here and there. But there is a definite and noticeable favouring of the sorts of Otherworldly scenery that correlates with the places in our own world people tend to say we are most likely to find Themselves as well. Many pagans talk of Fairy as if it were one vast forest or Europe stuck in medieval times.

There's a couple problems with that in my opinion that are worth addressing. First of all, I'm always wary of anything that narrows our understanding of Fairy rather than expanding it. The more restricted any view of the Otherworld is the quicker we will be faced with unmanageable contradictions. Secondly this is problematic because when we look at the evidence we do have from folklore and earlier anecdotal evidence we find that by and large people who went into Fairy found it to include not only the aforementioned wilderness but also cities, and usually the places people visited were either much like the ones on Earth or similar to what had existed within living memory. Or put another way people discussing going to Fairy a hundred years ago weren't usually seeing medieval villages[13] but rather described places just like they had left on Earth or places reminiscent of their grandparents or great-grandparents times. This is also what we generally see in descriptions of clothing as we previously discussed, with the Good People being described as wearing either contemporary fashions or those a generation or two out of date[14]. I think that the wider community would do well to seriously re-assess how Fairy is being imagined and why, and consider broadening horizons.

We have stories of fairies having their own cities in the Otherworld as well, showing that they are not inherently averse to cities as a concept. These cities are described as contemporaneous or only slightly antiquated by the humans who experienced them and seem to be very similar to their human counterparts at the time. Certainly enough so that the observer recognizes the place as a city and describes it as such. Briggs mentions one story of a shepherd who joined a fairy dance and was taken to a large palace, and there are similar accounts of large fairy habitations or cities in mythology and ballad material. There are specific types of fairies that are solitary beings, in folklore, but there are also many that are not – what Briggs calls 'trooping fairies' – and it seems logical that some of the social fairies would live together in towns and cities just as humans do.

Now for myself a large part of my personal practice is predicated on Journeying or being taken in trance or dreams to Fairy. I haven't spoken too much about this because by and large these are personal experiences and I don't think sharing them is necessary or adds value to the wider dialogue. However, in this case I'd like to share a few instances where places were visited that were neither wild nor primitive as I think my own anecdotal accounts have bearing here.

- There is a place I have been to on several occasions which I think of as a kind of 'Grand Central Station' although there are no trains there. It is a multi-level building, stone with a lot of brass or bronze fixtures and what seem to be electric lights, with large archways that lead off from a main area. There are clocks everywhere and glass windows. It seems to act as a transfer point where people can choose their destination and then pass through an archway to find the road that will take them there.

- I have stayed in a place that is very much like a small modern house, with running water, indoor plumbing, and a functional kitchen. The only thing that wasn't entirely modern was that it was heated by a fireplace. Otherwise though, what acted at least like electric lights, a stove and refrigerator, all the usual comforts.

There have also been accounts of people today experiencing or seeing cities in Fairy, in dreams or visionary experiences. These accounts like the older folkloric ones describe places that are contemporary or only slightly out of date to what we have today. Several of us have also experienced, separately, something like a train station that seems to allow people to go to different destinations in the Otherworld. At the least I think we can safely say that not all fairies are technophobes or luddites and that cities in Fairy make as much sense as they do in the human world, and probably exist for the same reasons. Several cities in the Otherworld that I have experienced seem distinctly modern, with paved roads, traffic lights, and a mix of residential, entertainment, and business areas. None of these are uniform but like places on earth they each have their own personality – one reminded me a bit of some older New England cities where the buildings seemed older than the overall energy of the place, while another was very sleek and modern and had a very rushed feel to it as if everything was in motion. Not to disabuse anyone's idealized ideas of what Fairy might be but these were not perfect versions of cities either, they had some shady looking beings (not unique to cities by any means) hanging around, there was rubbish in the streets and by the buildings, and one consisted of nothing but one-way streets.

I have, of course, also been to places that were wilderness, and places that reminded me of human habitations from various time periods – but then again, I've been to the same variety of places in this world as well. I know some people feel that whatever we see or experience in Fairy reflects our own expectations but I disagree; I have often seen things I didn't understand and so couldn't reflect an expectation and sometimes have pointedly not gotten what I expected. I rather loathe cities myself and if I were to expect one in Fairy, I would probably imagine it either as an ideal small city or some sort of perfect past vision of an early modern city and that is definitely not what I have experienced. I will also admit that I haven't seen anything resembling cars myself in the places I've been even though I would expect them in settings that seem so modern but I have seen a lot of metal work in bronze and various alloys. I also haven't seen any guns. That isn't to say there aren't any motor vehicles or modern weapons there, just that I haven't personally experienced them.

I suspect that our relationship with the world of Fairy and the relationship of its inhabitants with us is far more intrinsic and symbiotic than we realize. Perhaps the way that time moves differently between us affects our perceptions of this but it seems clear that there is a mimicry that occurs either intentionally or coincidentally, or even because of the influx of humans to Fairy. Perhaps it comes from their own observations and visits among us in this world. It is safe to assume I think that this pattern which has occurred across folklore into the 20th century is not about to stop now. What my experiences have convinced me of is that Fairy is a stunningly diverse place and we shouldn't underestimate that.

Another major shift that we see moving into the 20th and 21st centuries is a shifting of Fairy out of a separate world and into our own human world. This view is intrinsically married to a shift in some demographics to seeing fairies wholly as nature spirits.

When many people today conceptualize the world of Fairy, they imagine a romanticized, anachronistic version of our human world hundreds of years ago. This is doubtless because most of the accounts we have in writing are from past centuries and describe a world which seemed out of synch with the contemporary world, usually a few decades or more behind whatever humans of the time were doing. However, if we look not at the accounts themselves to describe Fairyland but at the pattern they show of the relationship and synchronization of the two worlds we might suggest a different conclusion for imagining Fairy today. What we would expect to see, if the pattern holds true, is some areas which may indeed be very different from our own or reflective of our own deep past but also many that would appear almost identical to modern earth or of human towns and cities of the 20th century.

Chapter 4

Things Change, Things Stay the Same

Having looked at fairies in the modern world and at Fairy itself in a modern context now I'd like to explore some ways that the older folklore about fairies remains constant. Some of this involves looking at modern popular ideas that some people would argue are examples of evolution but when examined don't make functional sense and some look at ways that modern encounters still reflect older ones. I think we need to have an understanding of this balance, that while fairies do change, they are also changing from a place of growth the way humans which follows a logic progression and incorporates the history into the new.

Plastic, Iron, and Warding Off Fairies

This was originally discussed in one of my blogs but I think it's important to include it here as well, because it is such a good example of the way that some newer beliefs seem good on the surface but just don't hold up when examined.

I've run across the idea several times in the last few years, based as far as I'm aware on something from fiction, that fairies are now averse to plastic instead of iron. I've seen several iterations of this but the general concept seems to be rooted in the idea that fairies were averse to iron because it was unnatural or foreign and that plastic is more unnatural or new and unnatural so therefore, now, they would be averse to plastic and not iron. There is the additional idea with this that fairies have overcome their aversion to iron, adjusted to the metal, or developed a resistance to it.

The idea of fairies being scared off by iron because it's new human technology goes back to the late Victorian period and can be found in such popular works as 'The Fairy Faith In Celtic

Countries'. It is a concept that hinges on the idea that fairies, as Otherworldly beings, do not exist but rather were primitive misunderstandings of so-called real world phenomena, in this case folk memories or early interactions between different cultural groups or groups with different technology. More specifically this theory was usually explained as meetings between bronze-wielding people and invaders with iron weapons where the bronze-carrying people fled in terror from the new metal. Basically fairies being afraid of iron because it was a new-fangled human tech was a late 19th- early 20th century way of euhemerizing fairies. There is no actual evidence of any sort to support the idea and it's been largely discredited among modern scholars. It is still repeated in some places because it can be found in print sources and is in many, many public domain works. And as we've already discussed there's a lot of material supporting that fairies were drawn to and likely to borrow modern human technology, which immediately contradicts the idea they'd be historically averse to it.

The idea of plastic being a replacement for iron to ward against fairies seems to have sprung from fiction and some questions relating to RPGs. The core idea behind people developing the concept as I've seen it is that if fairies were averse to iron because it represented new human technology then plastic as 20th century human tech should naturally freak the Good Folk out. Sort of an a = b logic.

Related is the idea that fairies have suddenly developed a resistance or immunity to iron, making it ineffective, although this one seems to rely simply on iron beings so common that people assume fairies must have gotten used to it by now. This theory goes that having become immune to iron they are now averse to plastic.

Where the idea immediately begins to fall apart is the overlap between plastic use and continued stories of fairies being warded off by iron. Plastic has been around since 1907 but stories of fairies avoiding iron persist into the 21st century, and there're no new accounts in folklore or anecdotes of them avoiding plastic. It also must be noted that plastic is nearly ubiquitous and can even be found in most clothing not to mention at the bottom of the ocean and in places without human habitations. Humans have made plastic a real plague in this world. Meaning that if fairies were really averse to plastic, we would have already entirely driven the Good Folk out of the human world.

The other aspect to fairies now fearing or being warded off by plastic is based on fairies being nature spirits in the most literal sense, and so averse to anything 'unnatural'. From this view fairies would embrace anything organic and reject anything chemically produced with plastic as the easy target given its high profile for lack of composting. Fairies as nature spirits leans into the idea that fairies are a sort of environmental noble savage trope with wings. Fairies, in toto, as nature spirits is another complicated discussion however. The idea, which is widespread in American paganism and elsewhere now, comes from an outgrowth of concepts shaped in theosophy and Victorian art and fiction and is widely at odds with folkloric understandings of fairies which are complex and nuanced.

Based on folklore and living cultural belief, iron is the most ubiquitous protection against fairies. It isn't because iron is 'unnatural' but because some fairies can't seem to stand the metal itself in any form, which is why steel also works. We can find references across written and oral folklore to fairies being averse to iron and steel, in multiple cultures, up through today.

The why of this often isn't discussed in depth among people who believe in it just as the effectiveness of turning clothes inside out to break being pixy-led isn't, because people care more that it works rather than why exactly it works. When it is discussed it's more theoretical guesses by people because no one really does know for certain. What we can say for certain is that it's a well-documented belief and one with history to it.

Of course, not all fairies are warded off by iron because nothing applies equally to all fairies. Some are warded off by salt, or rowan, or Christian prayers and symbols. The Good People are a diverse lot. And perhaps there are those that are averse to plastic just as there are those that we might categorize as nature spirits, even though it doesn't apply to the majority

I must admit I am unsure why the focus here is on plastic specifically and not, say, modern mass-produced foods which have lots of chemical additives but people don't hesitate to use as offerings. It seems to be a case of picking and choosing based on a person's own inclinations.

I would be very cautious about embracing the idea of fairies being afraid of or warded off by plastic without giving careful thought to how much plastic actually is around you at all times. Just as many people aren't aware of what is and isn't iron around them, people are rarely aware of how much plastic surrounds them constantly.

That all said what's the deal with fairies and iron anyway and how does that work in the modern world? Folklore about the Othercrowd stretches back centuries, with much of the recorded material we have focusing on protection against them and often recommending iron, although in the modern world I see a great deal of confusion on the subject and related topics. In that context here are some key points:

1. Apotropaic Iron – Iron is said in folklore to protect against a wide range of spirits and negative magics including many of the Good Neighbors and Alfar, Ghosts, Demons, and witches. Iron objects deter the majority of the Other Crowd who are averse to its presence and things like knives, scissors, nails, and horseshoes were recommended as protective objects. It is said that cemeteries had iron fences to contain any ghosts inside. Similarly older folklore said that demons were also repelled by iron, and it was believed to break the magic of witches. A horseshoe hung up above a doorway kept out a wide range of spirits as well as protecting from baneful magic.

There is no set understanding of why iron works for this, but the belief is very widespread.

2. Fairies and Iron – Across Western European folklore, particularly in the Celtic language speaking cultures and the Germanic cultures, we find the idea that iron is an ideal protection against Otherworldly beings. There is no agreement whether this must be blacksmith forged iron or any form of iron, but as mass production has come in since the industrial revolution there seems to be no indication that iron in any form is less effective. In fact we do have British accounts claiming that railways and trains drove off the Good People as they came into new areas, something that is also attributed to iron church bells; while we can argue about whether the iron here was the crucial feature as opposed to the sound, it does at least support that mass produced iron can be associated with protection.

It's always best to remember that fairy is a general term, like animal, that applies to a wide array of beings. Iron is recommended as a superlative protection against fairies, but there will always be those who are not bothered by it. If we were to say that about 80% of fairies can't bear the touch of iron then the other 20% have no problem with it, and those would include mine faeries, forge spirits, and some house spirits; basically any fairy that would naturally exist or dwell near iron or iron ore. Also any of the aos sidhe connected to smithing don't seem to be bothered by iron.

3. Iron or Steel? – Iron is hard to come by these days and although it is the best protection steel will also work in a pinch. Steel is between 90 and 98% iron depending on the alloy, so a steel object is obviously mostly an iron object. Iron and steel are effectively the same substance and have been treated that way in folklore and for apotropaic purposes historically, where we find references to both iron and steel being used to ward off fairies. Generally the type of item isn't as important as the material in this case so anything made of iron that you can procure can be used for protective purposes. In tradition any worked iron can be used to ward against fairies including iron weapons, iron nails, iron horse shoes, iron scissors, iron fire tongs, etc. There's no indication in folklore or anecdotal material that the form of the iron matters, only its presence. There is debate about whether it has to be hand worked iron or not, and I doubt that will ever be settled, but we have accounts of non-hand forged being used successfully.

So to sum up, steel has the same effect as iron because steel is almost identical to iron in substance. Or put another way steel, while it has some other metals alloyed in it, is still mostly iron.

4. Cold Iron – Many people are familiar with the term 'cold iron' and associate it today with pure or simply worked forged iron – what is technically called 'pig iron' or 'crude iron'. There are also some who draw on role playing games to understand this concept and believe that cold iron is iron that was cold forged. While interesting these are decidedly modern views on the concept, relying in part on technology that didn't exist when some of the older references to cold iron were made. Historically the term cold iron was a poetic term for any iron weapon and is synonymous today with the term 'cold steel'. 'Grose's 1811 Dictionary of the Vulgar Tongue' defines cold iron as *"A sword, or any other weapon for cutting or stabbing"*; in modern parlance cold steel would refer to a gun or similar weapon. When you see a reference to cold iron it is talking about an iron weapon, usually a sword or knife.

5. Using Iron – There are several ways to use iron to protect yourself and your home from fairies, if it's needed. Lady Wilde suggested protecting infants from being taken as changelings by sewing a bit of iron into the hem of the child's clothes (Wilde, 1888). I was taught a modern version of this, where it was recommended that a steel safety pin be attached to a child's clothing, particularly sleepwear. Another commonly recommended protection for children and babies was to hang a pair of scissors, opened into the shape of a cross, above the cradle (Briggs, 1976). A horseshoe can be hung up over the door way, points up, which not only acts to ward off fairies but is also said to draw good luck. An iron knife or cross is also an excellent protection, either carried or hung up above the door or bed (Briggs, 1976). Robert Kirk in his 1691 treatise on the Good Neighbours mentions the practice of putting *"bread, the Bible, or a piece of iron"* in the bed of a woman giving birth to protect the infant from being stolen. In Welsh belief a knife, particularly of iron, was so effective a protection that should friendly fairies visit a home all knives were hidden from sight lest they be offended and if a traveling person was attacked by the Othercrowd he had only to pull his blade for them to disappear (Sikes, 1880). Another method found in Germanic and Norse traditions is to hammer an iron nail into a post near the doorway or alternately part of the door frame. Additionally it is said to be as effective to draw a circle using an iron nail or knife around what you want to protect (Gundarsson, 2007).

A more modern, but still useful method, is the use of iron water. Fill a small spray bottle with water and add iron filings, iron dust, or a piece of iron, and allow to sit for a few days. The water can be sprayed into a room or around the home as needed.

As always keep in mind that the use of iron will not affect all fairies, as some – including mine fairies and house fairies – are not bothered by it. For those that are sensitive to it, though, it is a superlative protection.

To summarize; ultimately the amount doesn't seem to matter as long as the content is iron. The shape is also not important although it is more often recommended in a form that is sharp – a knife or nail – or combined with a holy symbol like a cross. The placement is best either on the person or very close by, especially near where they are sleeping. When placed above or next to an entrance it is believed that the presence of iron will keep out any Otherworldly beings. Although in today's world iron may be more difficult to find steel is fairly easily obtained and will work as well.

6. Fairies and Blood – There is an idea I have occasionally run across that the Good People would be or are averse to human blood because it contains iron. There are some anecdotal accounts which claim fairies have white blood and are averse to or avoid the colour red and human blood (see: 'Fairy Faith in Celtic Countries' and 'The Good People' for more on this). However, these are late 19th century and 20th century accounts which hinge on the Catholic belief that fairies have white blood because they are not mortal and have been denied Heaven/salvation and they avoid human blood not because it contains iron as some people are now alleging but because it represents the afterlife they are barred from. We also have a multitude of evidence that red is a colour associated with fairies and that many fairies are known to wear red which contradicts the idea that they would avoid that colour. While there is at least one anecdotal account, recorded by Lysaght in 'The Good People', of a belief that the Good Folk were averse to the colour red and to blood, we see far more stories of fairies eating red meat, cooking bread with blood[15], and in some cases eating humans even the ones who are averse to iron, so it doesn't seem like blood and forged or ferrous iron have the same effect.

Further to that point, the iron in human blood, aka haemoglobin, is not the kind that would ward against fairies anyway. Iron in human blood is a very miniscule amount; there's only something like 4 grams total in a grown man altogether including blood, bone marrow, etc., Second of all haemoglobin is chemically different from ferrous iron which almost certainly makes a difference. In short – iron or steel in any form protects against fairies. Human blood does not.

7. **Modern Iron** – There was an interesting conversation I had with a friend about the possible apotropaic qualities of steel body jewellery against fairies. It reminded me that many people are unaware of how pervasive iron, iron alloys, and ferrous oxide are (in the US). To wrap this section up I wanted to offer a few examples of some of the unexpected places iron shows up (besides the aforementioned jewellery):

- There is ferrous iron in flour, so in almost all breads, pastas, and baked goods – vegetarian and vegan inclusive.
- There is ferrous oxide in almost all tinted makeup and definitely in all dark makeup.
- It's in some medical products like calamine lotion.
- It's found in several tattoo dyes.
- And, of course, the more obvious larger scale uses for iron and steel like cookware, silverware, grocery carts...

Fairy Help, Fairy Harm

I want to wrap this chapter up by discussing the way that fairies have been consistent in their interactions with humans across folklore and into modern experiences and anecdotes. I think this is an important issue to touch on precisely because it is an aspect of fairies that is often misunderstood or confused in modern contexts or downplayed.

Modern paganism, and perhaps more broadly mainstream Western culture, seems to constantly be trapped in a mobius strip argument about the potential help or harm caused by fairies. There is one side that argues, staunchly, that the Good Folk are entirely benevolent and benign to humans. In contrast there is another side that argues just as fervently that the Othercrowd should be entirely avoided and warded against because of the danger they represent. And then there's the people, like myself, who argue for a kind of middle ground that acknowledges the very tangible dangers but also the potential advantages to fairies. When in doubt, however, always act with caution and keep the risk in mind because there are serious and sometimes permanent consequences.

What I want to do here is look at the evidence we have for both sides in folklore. I think too often people, especially outside places that have maintained some degree of belief in these beings, rely entirely on their own personal experiences and perceptions. I'm not saying to ignore your own experiences, of course, but I am suggesting that one person's experiences don't a body of lore make. I have never drowned, for example, but I fully believe that people who go swimming may drown under various conditions – because I know that my personal experiences are not the sum total of the subject. Hopefully the following material will provide a wider view.

First let's look at a few examples of fairy help. These are harder to find in the source material and often come from folk tales rather than folklore, which should be noted. This may be because there have long been prohibitions in many cultures that believe in these beings that to brag or boast of the good, they might do a human will result in that goodness being revoked. This extends to talking about a wide array of fairy interference in one's life including having a leannán sidhe [fairy lover] or learning from them. That all said:

1. Healing physical maladies. This can include both illnesses and deformities. There is a very famous story, often repeated sometimes under the title of 'Lushmore', of a man with a hunchback in Ireland who was passing a fairy fort, heard the fairies singing, politely joined in and was reward by having his back healed. Several versions of the tale can be found on the

Duchas.ie site, but one example:

> *He heard the fairies singing – Monday, Tuesday. The man said*
> *Monday Tuesday and Wednesday. The fairies ran up to the man*
> *and asked him to teach them that song. The man taught them the*
> *song. The fairies asked him that gift die he want he said to take*
> *the hump off his back. The man went home without the hump.*
> (Duchas, entry 453).

2. Help with work. There are accounts of fairies doing work for humans they like. Often there isn't any reason given to explain why they liked that person, as we see in this example:

> *This man was supposed to have something to do with the fairies.*
> *The fairies used to do all the work for him at night time.* (Duchas, entry 246).

3. Money – in one late 19th century story an Irish Fairy king helps a man about to be evicted pay his rent by giving him gingerbread made to look like gold. The man is told to get a receipt when he pays, which he does, so that when the gold turns back to gingerbread the next day, he can't be held accountable. This story is in line with wider tales of fairies giving money or support to people they favour or take pity on.

4. Removing curses. In the ballad of Alison Gross a man who has been cursed by a witch is rescued by the Queen of the Seely court who removes the curse. I have also had what I would describe as blessing experiences, including the apparently miraculous healing of my middle child's back deformity, and I do think it is important to understand that the Good Folk can interact in a positive way with people and do so in the world today. The possibility of positive results, however, should not negate the dangers.

Now that we've established the Good Neighbours can be helpful let's look at a fraction of the evidence that they can represent risk to humans. I have seen some people try to argue that all of these examples are either propaganda from those antithetical to fairies or the result of people with the wrong mindset who expected bad and so got it. I want to say this as nicely as I can: the entirety of folklore and many, many people's modern experiences are not lies or wrong because a person doesn't happen to like the way they depict fairies. If we look beyond western Europe and the diaspora we can find a multitude of examples from other cultures, including those that are still non-Christian, of equally dangerous or ambivalent spirit beings. I am actually not aware of any culture that has only benevolent spirits in their belief system, so it strikes me as extremely odd to view fairies that way.

In the below examples we will be looking strictly at direct harm caused to humans in the human world by fairies. One can argue that such things as fairy abductions and possession also qualify as harm but those topics are nuanced and deserve a fuller discussion than what we will be doing here.

1. Causing deformities. In point 1 above I mentioned fairies straightening a man's back in a story; that story ends with another man similarly afflicted trying the same cure and getting twice the hunch on his back for his efforts:

The fairies did not like his song and instead of taking the hump off him they put the other man's hump on him and the man went home with two humps. (Duchas, entry 454).

Briggs attributes anything that deforms or warps the human body to possible invisible fairy blows or injuries, particularly issues of the joints or spine.

2. Killing or sickening livestock. Fairies are very well known for afflicting domestic animals, especially cows. This was sometimes called 'elf-struck' or 'elf-shot' and may be marked by a mark or lump on the animal to indicate where it was struck (Narvaez, 1991). Accounts of this can be found in the Duchas.ie archives describing the results:

> Also we are told that fairies used to shoot cows, when the cows would "graze on a "gentle" spot. We call a place "gentle" when it is supposed to belong to fairies. A "shot" cow became weak and would not eat. (Duchas, entry 231).

3. Exhausting people nearly to death. There is another account on Duchas of a man who saw the fairies hurling in a field and went to join them only to be kept playing until he almost died of exhaustion. In folklore we find tales of fairies making people dance until they collapse or die.

4. They will kill you. There are many accounts of fairies physically harming or just directly killing people for offenses, so much so that Patricia Lysaght says:

> That physical disability or even death can result from interference with fairy property such as a rath is well attested in Irish tradition. Many examples are evident... (Narvaez, 1991, p 45).

These are often related to harm a human has done to a fairy place or fairy tree. However, sometimes it's just because the person offended them by breaking the fairies' rules of etiquette, as in this example where death was threatened for trying to join a fairy song:

> All the fairies went in to Harvey's fort, and they began singing and dancing and inside in the fort. One of the men had a fiddle and he began to play a tune the fairies were playing One of the fairies came

out of the fort and told the man that if he played that tune again he would kill him and the man ran home as fast as he could. (Duchas, entry 75).

Even into the 21st century there are stories of people dying after damaging fairy trees.

5. Blinding. The fairies are known to blind people, something that is found as a staple in the 'Midwife to the Fairies' stories where a midwife who accidently touches her eye with fairy ointment lets slip that she can see them and is blinded or has her eye put out. An anecdotal account from late 20th century Newfoundland describes a man harassed by fairies who is eventually blinded by them (Narvaez, 1991). There is an account on the Duchas site of a fiddler who refused fairy food and was blinded in one eye by an angry fairy woman.

6. Tumours. Multiple accounts support victims of a fairy blast or fairy wind suffering from immediate and inexplicable swellings which are found to be tumours; there are also anecdotal accounts of people with these swellings where random objects like bones, grass, or straw are found inside them (Narvaez, 1991).

7. Madness or loss of cognitive abilities or speech. Anecdotal accounts from Yeats 'Celtic Twilight' to Narvaez's 'Newfoundland Berry Pickers in the Fairies' discuss the fairies driving people mad or taking away their cognitive function. Narvaez also discusses accounts of encounters which resulted in speech impairment and there are folktales of fairies taking a person's speech entirely something that is also discussed by Emma Wilby in relation to a Scottish witch who dealt with fairies.

8. Strokes. The term stroke for a cerebral accident or aneurysm comes from the term 'fairy stroke' or 'elf stroke' and the idea that a blow from the Good Folk could cause this physical issue. Briggs mentions this as a method used by the fairies to steal humans and livestock, but the concept behind it is also mentioned as kind of fairy punishment in 'The Good People' anthology. Paralysis is also attributed to fairy anger in some cases (Briggs, 1976). Alaric Hall discusses elf-shot at length in his book, and mentions its use on humans and animals as well as its usually permanent effects on a person. elf stroke in itself is a complicated subject and being shot by the fairies can have multiple effects on a person including many of the other issues listed here.

9. Bruising and Muscle Cramps. On the mildest end, fairies are known to pinch, hit, and otherwise assault humans resulting in bruising and cramping (Briggs, 1976). The fairies are not averse to beating a person into cooperating as we see in an account by Wilby relating to a Scottish witch reluctant to do what the fairies were asking her; they are also not averse to beating a person because they want to, as we find in an account on Duchas, where a man who sees the fairies and acknowledges that he can see them is attacked and beaten nearly to death by them.

I also want to include some anecdotal examples, both my own experiences and those that have been shared with me to demonstrate that this isn't all just old stories:

Blindness – going temporarily blind for not doing what the fairies ask. This happened to me for three days once.
Madness – driving a person crazy to try to force compliance on an issue. I have had people come to me for help more than once because of this issue.
Physical marks – ranging from bruising to scratching. I've experienced it, my friends have experienced it, people coming me asking for advice have talked about it. This one is pretty common.

Trying to Kill Someone – I have heard a few accounts of the Fair Folk causing serious bodily harm bordering on near death. In one case this involved a person's car inexplicably moving out of gear and running them over while they stood in front of it.

There is a reason that all cultures which believe in the Good Neighbours have so very many protections against them and such caution in dealing with them, and it's important to remember that this aspect of fairies still remains in the 21st century as much as it did in the past.

Chapter 5

21st Century Encounters

Anecdotal evidence is not limited to a hundred years ago – it still exists today. We have the strangest habit as a culture (speaking especially of Americans here) of giving some credit to people a hundred years ago for actually possibly having had some genuine experience of the Otherworld while simultaneously doing everything possible to rationalize away people in our time saying the same things. We can believe that a hundred years ago someone saw or experienced Fairy, but simultaneously believe that no one can really have those same experiences today except intangibly in dreams or meditations. And yet people do still see and experience Fairy as they always have; we are just more reluctant to talk about it today because of the strength of the disbelief. Not to say we should immediately believe every claim by every person, because discernment is always valuable under any circumstances, but I'd caution against deciding that our own cynicism should be the measure for everyone. What we personally see or understand is not the limit or ability of everyone else. It may be best to find a balance between a healthy scepticism and an attitude that espouses, as Shakespeare said that *"there are more things on Heaven and earth than are dreamt of in your philosophy"*. There have been some efforts to collect modern anecdotes, such as 'Seeing Fairies' by Marjorie Johnson and Simon Young as well as an excellent documentary 'The Fairy Faith – In Search of Fairies'. These modern collections are just as important as the older ones because they show that the beliefs are still vital and alive, if less visible.

Ultimately anecdotal evidence is important because it gives us a snapshot of the beliefs of the people at different points of time. It shows us not only what they believed but in practical terms how they felt the different worlds interacted and affected each other. Reading a range of anecdotal evidence across different periods of time is important, and for those interested in fairylore it's essential to see the beliefs in different areas and the changes to beliefs over time. We can learn a great deal from this material, if we are willing to embrace the older as well as the new.

In this chapter I would like to share several of my own personal modern encounters. I have talked about these previously in other places but I feel like it's important to include them here if only to illustrate the types and range of things that modern fairy experiences can cover. I had contemplated including other people's experiences as well but ultimately, I am uncomfortable speaking for other people in this area. I do highly encourage readers to check out the online Fairy Census which includes a wide range of modern fairy encounters by many different people in a variety of places. Here I can only speak for myself and my own experiences.

Yes, these did all really happen, and in some cases other people witnessed them and can verify. Yes, many of these did happen in the US. Yes, I am sure these involved beings I would call 'Good Neighbours'. For those who regularly read my writing or attend workshops I teach some of these may not be new. I am writing this to show people that interactions with the Fair Folk do still happen, and that those interactions are not always what some views of the 'fairies' may lead us anticipate. I shall try to organize these somewhat by topic.

Pixy-led

I've experienced being pixy-led several times in my life. This phenomena occurs when a person gets lost or is led astray in what should be familiar territory and is believed to be the result of fairy magic. I will include a few stories here.

Many years ago I had a loose assortment of friends who were all different types of pagans. One full moon we decided to get together and have a ritual and one woman mentioned a spot out in the woods that she had used many times. We all met up in early afternoon and then drove out to the suburban home where her parents lived, before hiking back into the woods about a mile or so. The ritual location was lovely and we had a casual ceremony followed by a long, pleasant conversation that lasted into the early evening. Finally it was full dark, and even with the full moon above us the forest was closing in so we packed up and started back. After walking for about five minutes we could clearly see the lights from the houses shining through the trees ahead of us. But after ten more minutes the lights were no closer. We climbed over rocks and around trees, through thorns and fallen branches, yet never seemed able to move forward. One other friend and I began to suspect fairy enchantment, as the rest of the group fought to push forward. Finally, after perhaps another 15 minutes of walking, my friend and I acknowledged that we were being pixy-led; we began to laugh and compliment the fairies on such a fine joke. The energy broke with an almost physical snap and within a few minutes we emerged in a backyard a few houses down from where we'd first gone into the woods.

Another time I was at the cairns at Sliabh na Caillighe (Loughcrew) with a group and I had wandered a bit off by myself. Despite the space being relatively small, fenced in, and marked by cairns scattered across the landscape I found myself disoriented and unable to find my way – I literally kept wandering in circles around one specific set of stones. Even though I was there with a dozen other people absolutely no one was around me. It was, quite frankly, unnerving. I finally stopped fighting against it took a moment to pour out a bit of water as an offering and ask – nicely – to be allowed to leave. A moment later I walked forward and immediately found the path down the hill and several of my friends.

Healing

When I was in Iceland I fell ill and was worried about what I should do, being in a foreign country and on a tour at the time. That day we were staying at a Bed and Breakfast and I went out to wander around the grounds; I was having a lot of odd experiences including hearing footsteps behind me on the empty trail. I felt guided to walk off the path and ended up in a very odd little hollow area where I did some meditative work. That night I went to bed feeling badly enough that I had decided I'd ask the woman running the tour to take me into the closest town the next day to either get some medicine or find a doctor. I woke up around 3 am from a dead sleep, drenched in sweat, to see three figures standing around my bed. They looked somewhat human, tall, thin, wearing long dresses (from what I could make out in the low light of the room). One stood to each side of the bed and one at the foot. I should have been frightened but I wasn't; I felt an odd sort of acceptance about the whole thing and went back to sleep. I was perfectly fine when I woke up in the morning and to this day, I'm convinced that I was healed by whatever visited me.

Fairy Borrowing

My friend has had a large shrine/altar for the aos sidhe in her store for 15 years. One equinox we needed to move the shrine, which was an epic undertaking, and took most of a morning. Several days later I noticed a fluorite ring was missing from a jewellery display. We both assumed it had been stolen, which was upsetting, but is an unfortunate reality in retail. Then my friend found it, days later on the new fairy shrine – covered in years of dust as if it had been there for a long time. (note we left it there – if they want an offering enough to take it, they can keep it)

Another time I was helping out in my friend's store and I looked down and realized my wedding ring was gone. I panicked and my friend and I searched everywhere but there was no

51

trace of it. I made several offerings to the aos sidhe hoping the ring would turn up, because I knew of their tendency to take jewellery, but it didn't. Months went by and I felt pressed to write my Fairy Witchcraft book, which I did (separate story). Shortly after I finished the book and submitted it to my publisher my friend found the ring sitting in front of her altar.

Dangerous encounters

Many years ago I was hiking in a local state park known by some to have a strong presence of the Good People to it. In this same place I'd been pixy-led while I was with a friend, and I know of at least one other person who had also been pixy-led there. This particular day I decided to go off trail at the bottom of the waterfall and hike around the rocky area near the water's edge. I came around a place where the rockface had jutted out and into a small secluded area with a little pool. I stopped; in the pool was a pale, dark haired woman (not human). She was about waist deep in the water and had been running her fingers through her hair when I walked around the cliff. There was a strong feeling of menace in the air that made my hair stand on end. She looked at me. I looked at her. She told me to get out. I backed up and left the way I'd come as fast as I could.

We have a fairy thorn in my yard – which is its own story, actually. Anyway, one day while doing yard work my husband damaged the tree accidentally. He came in and told me and I was very upset (read; freaked out) and told him to go make an offering right away. I went out myself and offered honey and milk, and asked him if he had had done but he was still in the middle of mowing the lawn. I emphasized he needed to do it as soon as possible. So a week or so goes by and it's around seven one morning. I'm up with my son who was an infant at the time while everyone else is still sleeping when we hear the most Gods-awful loud crashing noise. I rush to the window with the baby and looking down at the driveway see that a roughly

20 foot long branch from an oak tree has impaled my husband's car. I go wake him up, and the first thing I say is something like "Did you make that offering to the fairies like I told you to?" and he says "No I thought you'd done it for me.". So I say, "Oh no. You should have done your own. You'd better go see what's happened to your car." The car was totalled, by the way.

Positive Encounters

There's twice at least that I believe the Good People have saved my home or my life one way or another. The first time I was in my living room, getting ready to go run some errands when I caught sight of something moving on the wall behind the television, by the outlet where the electronics are plugged in. I walked part way across the room, but there wasn't anything there. I stood for a minute or so, nothing happened, so I went and sat back down. Glancing over the same thing happened again, but I ignored it. The third time it was the more distinctive form of a small person moving back and forth in front of the outlet, so I got up again and walked over this time right up to the outlet. The figure disappeared but a few seconds later the largest cord plugged into the outlet sparked and then started burning. Because I was standing right next to it, I had time to pull it out of the wall before anything else caught fire, and the only damage was the cord itself, melted and burned (also probably added some white to my hair).

I have had many strange experiences with the Othercrowd relating to butterflies and moths, and one relates to saving my life. Several years ago just before going to bed I started to have a severe allergic reaction to something (for which I now have an EpiPen, by the way). I was going into anaphylactic shock, which as a former EMT I recognized, but at the time I was scared and made the very irrational decision not to disturb my husband. I went to bed, with my tongue swelling and each breath a struggle. Suddenly my husband jumped up yelling and turned on the light. He swore that a huge moth had just flown, forcefully, into his face, although he could find no evidence of any moth anywhere. A sense of calm came over me and I told him to call 911 and explained that I needed help. And obviously I lived, although I'll admit things got a bit dicey on the ambulance ride.

Miscellaneous

One midsummer I was celebrating with several friends. We were in the store one of my friend's owned and although it was closed and it was getting late, we had the door open for some fresh air. As the three of us were cleaning up a large – perhaps book sized – moth flew in and was hovering near the ceiling by the front windows. My friend who owned the shop saw a large white moth. Our other friend and myself saw a small man with moth wings. Our other friend finally pointed out and said, loudly, 'You!' and the creature dropped straight down into the front window display where it disappeared. We all searched for quite a while but never found any trace of it.

My household spirit has been seen by every member of my family although not always in the same way. Several of us have seen her as a girl around 12 years old, dressed in white, with long dark hair. One of my children has seen her as a light and another as a blur of pale motion. She tends to appear in hallways and doorways most often. She will also sometimes speak and has been heard by several people as well.

These are only a handful of experiences – I mentioned the two fairy hound sightings in a previous chapter as well – but I hope they illustrate some of the diversity in potential modern encounters.

Chapter 6

Cautions Moving Forward

If you are reading this book, I assume it is because this is a subject that interests you on some level and that this will not – and likely already is not – the only book you'll ever read about fairies. Which is exactly as it should be since we can only learn the layers of nuance around fairies by casting a very wide net in our studies. But just as there is and has always been a huge amount of diversity with this subject there is and always has been a lot of confusion and misinformation circulating as well. In this chapter I'd like to look at several important issues particular to modern fairies that require extra discernment.

Sources For Modern Beliefs
There will always be a tension between spiritual belief and fact because the two do not always go hand in hand. Of course, people will have a diverse array of sources for what they believe and why they believe that, and in our modern multi-cultural, multi-media world those sources are particularly diverse. But I have found that many people take a belief they run across, especially if it seems appealing to them, immediately as true and incorporate it into their belief system without digging into the core of the beliefs. It is important, though, to dig into that core because some of the beliefs floating around out there are a lot more problematic than they seem and may have sources that are far from actual folk belief and reflect ideas the person may be diametrically opposed to. I want to offer a few examples here for people to consider.

1. You will see some people suggesting that fairies' origins lie in the pre-Celtic or pre-Iron Age human populations of Ireland and

the UK; effectively, that when the new populations came in the older population fled into the wilder areas and became part of the new groups' folklore. This is an idea that was popular among scholars during the Victorian period but has fallen entirely out of vogue over the last hundred years, because there is absolutely no evidence to support it. Current theories and genetic studies support the idea that there was no massive population shift, rather there was an influx of new cultural influences which would make the idea of an older population being driven out by invaders impossible.

The theory is rooted in the racism that was common during that era, shown in the descriptions of these folk-memory peoples as either pygmies or small, dark, primitive people. In both cases the original materials that discuss this theory imply they were an earlier form of humans or a more primitive human race that fled at the contact with the new iron technology of the invaders. The utter lack of evidence to support any such thing happening is why the theory has been discarded, but unfortunately the popularity of public domain material has meant a revival of the idea among modern pagans, most of whom are not aware the racism layered into the concept.

2. Changeling folklore is extremely complex and layered. The Cliffs Notes version would be the idea that a human of any age is taken by the fairies to become one of their own and in place of the stolen human either a fairy or magically disguised object is left behind. Many popular changeling stories focus on infants or children being taken, and we can find a plethora of protective practices and objects used to prevent this, but there are also many changeling stories that feature an adult being taken, particularly women. There were various ways to diagnose a changeling and to force the fairies to return the real human; many of the methods of return were cruel or brutal and over the years resulted in multiple deaths. The case of Bridget Cleary is

perhaps the most famous.

It has become popular for some people to use the term changeling as a term of endearment for their children and for some people in the autistic community[16] to embrace the term as a self-identifier. The idea of doing so is apparently rooted in some late 20th century scholarship that sought to explain changelings as a misunderstanding by people of babies or children with autism. This idea, however, has an older history, coming from the Victorian attempt to explain changelings as a natural, not supernatural, phenomena.

Whereas modern theories focus on autism, the older versions focused on Down Syndrome and mental retardation, forwarding the racist, xenophobic, and ableist argument that changelings were examples of throwbacks to more primitive human races. The modern theories cannot, in my opinion, be separated from their historic sources as both original and modern seek to use a medical condition to offer an easy explanation for a complex and varied set of folk beliefs, and lean into the idea that a supernatural explanation for one medical condition could explain these beliefs.

Blaming autism now is not any more accurate than blaming Down Syndrome then, and both ignore the actual range of folk beliefs and variety of possible explanations outside the supernatural which would have encompassed a wide range of birth defects, medical issues, behavioural issues, and illnesses. In my opinion, embracing the idea from a spiritual perspective and romanticizing the idea by blending the belief in fairies as real with the idea that there is a human-world explanation for changelings endangers other already vulnerable populations by suggesting that humans with these conditions are not actually human. Which is exactly what led to so many deaths connected to these beliefs.

3. There is a subset of people who strongly feel that fae and fairy

have different meanings and represent different types of beings. The reality is that the words have the same general meaning; fae is the old French[17] predecessor of the English word fairy, and both mean an Otherworldly or enchanting being. Until very recently, and still in academia and folk belief, the two terms were used interchangeably as synonyms. Because of the divergence in meaning found in different groups now it is often helpful to take some time in a discussion to clarify how you are using the terms and ask how the other person uses them as well. It's always risky to assume we are all using these words the same way.

I will note one personal concern I have with this particular pair of terms, although this should be understood as my opinion. On the surface this belief may seem rather harmless and perhaps even an aspect of linguistic evolution – words do change meaning over time after all. Where the trouble comes in is that separating fae into the collective group and fairy into a specific being reinforces the post-modern rewriting of fairies from the dangerous and mercurial beings found in folklore into the twee beings of children's cartoons, perpetuating the minimalizing, disempowering, and redefining of fairies that began with the Victorians. It is another example of a dominant culture coming in, taking a belief from a non-dominant group, redefining it, and perpetuating it as the only accurate version.

4. Another issue that we often find is between folkloric fairies and the fairies of modern popular fiction. Many people who believe in fairies and even incorporate them into their spirituality draw not on folklore but on modern fiction as their sources. When I ask across social media for people's preferred or recommended fairy resources people often respond with fiction; the main names that come up are Holly Black, Jim Butcher, and LK Hamilton.

On the surface this may not seem like a problem and people often defend this by arguing these authors research into the folklore or are very accurate. However, the reality is that fiction is not meant to be accurate folklore and each of these authors forward ideas that are a problem in different ways. Holly Black's 'Modern Faerie Tales' series features a fairy changeling who grows up thinking she's human and only finds her real identity in her teens; this, of course, reinforces the idea that changelings are fairy babies who grow up human, rather than the depictions found in folklore which feature adult fairies disguised as babies, sickly fairy babies who subsequently die, and inanimate objects glamoured to look like the baby. Jim Butcher's 'Dresden Files' take a lot of liberties with the concepts of the fairy courts, add a third group (the wyld fae) and places English fairy queens in charge of traditionally Scottish fairy courts. LK Hamilton similarly alters folklore for plot, for example changing the idea of elfstruck from the traditional invisible arrows that cause wasting illnesses to a magically induced infatuation with one of the Sidhe after a sexual encounter with them.

In all these cases we see the actual, older folklore is being rewritten or reimagined for a plot point, which makes sense in fiction but contributes to the erosion of older folk beliefs. There is also an unpleasant layer of colonialism here, where people outside the cultures these beliefs come from are taking them and using them in a way that doesn't reflect the actual belief and results in those beliefs being radically changed by the dominant culture without concern for the culture being taken from.

Belief is and will always be a thing that resides more in the heart than the head. Because of this it can be difficult to unravel and release beliefs like those discussed above that people feel very strongly about, but which are built on problematic foundations. In fact it can seem harmless or even inconsequential to believe some of the things above, but the truth is that these examples are all things that are rooted in racism, ableism, xenophobia, and/or colonialism and we need to be aware of that and to try to work through and acknowledge when ideas we like reflect things we don't want to support. You can't say that you stand against racism, then forward beliefs rooted in that same concept. For our spirituality and spiritual beliefs to be healthy and holistic we must be willing to confront these things and untangle them from deeper beliefs and concepts.

Representation and Racism in Fairy Media

I've spoken out against racism in various areas, from Irish paganism to Heathenry to folklore, but one area that I've found it to be pervasive and often unaddressed relates to fairies, across 19th and 20th century folklore and into modern media. Despite diversity in folkloric accounts and anecdotal accounts when you ask most people in Western culture to describe a fairy or elf they don't usually picture a person of colour but often describe a fair skinned, usually blond, being.

An internet image search returns results that are mostly in line with the second idea and only a handful like the first. The covers of most urban fantasy books featuring fairies or elves also tend to largely show pale characters. Role playing games and the book series associated with them have historically played on the racist association of white with goodness and black with evil, giving us for example the black-skinned Drow elves who are described as being utterly evil and in thrall to an equally evil black-skinned spider goddess. This ingrained idea has created an environment that can be subtly or overtly unwelcoming to people of colour who are interested in fairies which is exactly why it must be addressed.

While there is a valid argument that anecdotal accounts in folklore often reflect the demographics of the populations experiencing them, folklore is a diverse and varied thing which also includes an array of beings that break out of any stereotype. We see Western European fairies with green skin as well as literal white, fairies that are blue, grey, red, and black. Anecdotal accounts into modern times reflect this as well with people mentioning seeing fairy beings with many different skin and hair colours. And, of course, fairies that are not human-shaped at all. Why then does popular culture persist in seeing fairies as normally light skinned and often fair haired? The short answer is that the Victorians had some ingrained notions of the [false] superiority of Western Europeans and their descendants over everyone else. This was expressed in fairylore through theories by scholars of the time that supposed the origins of fairies in primitive, dark, pygmy cultures and habitually depicted the more agrarian fairy beings as small and dark and the more noble fairies as tall, pale, and stereotypically Teutonic in appearance. This idea became embedded in the fiction that grew out of that time period, reflecting the author's biases and assumptions rather than older folklore and anecdotes.

We are starting to see an encouraging growth of diversity in artwork particularly on platforms like DeviantArt, but mainstream art lags behind. Still it's encouraging that imaginative fairy art is becoming more diverse and that images are getting out there that show fairies as more than just pretty white people in Renn Faire attire. In-roads have also been made in the realms of role playing games, with the recent move by Dungeons and Dragons to reclassify the so-called evil species and the idea of moral alignment so that morality and evil are completely removed from skin colour in game. Fiction has also started to show more variety in fairy depictions and to embrace the idea that this variety is a good thing.

Change can be a slow process but things are definitely moving in a better direction. Fairy fiction, comics, and role playing games are for everyone, as is a general interest in the subject, and the media we consume must reflect that. Hopefully going forward it will.

Pareidolia

There's been a trend in fairy groups for years of people posting pictures of what they claim are fairies caught on film. Usually these images are nature shots, with the alleged fairy appearing within and formed by the leaves and bark, or sometimes the images are blurry flying objects. People are often quick to jump in and comment that they can see the fairies in the picture occasionally even spotting new ones not seen by the person who took the picture.

Despite my own profound belief in fairies I am sceptical of these pictures and in my own experience most of them can be easily explained by natural phenomena or known factors and are examples of pareidolia. Discussing this, however, is usually not allowed or frowned on, as it's seen as discouraging belief or criticizing individual's experiences. My entire raison d'être is forwarding and encouraging belief in fairies[18] but I think it's essential to discuss pareidolia in relation to photos of fairies and understand how scepticism of these photos isn't the same as disbelief in fairies more generally.

Let's start by looking at what pareidolia is and the related phenomena of apophenia. Basically, pareidolia is the tendency for the human brain to see familiar shapes in random patterns, including faces, figures, and animals. We've all experienced this; for example, if you look at a wooden floor and find a face formed by the swirls and knots in the wood that's pareidolia. There have also been some very high-profile cases of pareidolia, such as when someone appears in a magazine because they have a piece of toast they claim looks like the Virgin Mary. Psychology uses pareidolia via the Rorschach test by having a person interpret a random ink blot and analysing the result.

The human brain is designed to recognize faces and shapes quickly as a survival mechanism, and its hardwired into the human brain to find faces in patterns. This is part of a process within the brain where if you are looking for a face or a person the portion of your brain responsible for that is activated and so you are naturally inclined to find what you are looking for – which is helpful in survival situations but not as much outside of them.

In other words, if you are looking for faces you are more likely to see faces. Apophenia is a related phenomenon where people will see or hear recognizable things in random input; pareidolia is considered a type of apophenia. Apophenia may play a role in ghost hunting via the interpretation of sounds and images. Pareidolia is a common phenomenon among all humans because it's how the human brain is wired to process patterns. In fairy groups, however, the phenomena isn't generally acknowledged, is in fact sometimes treated with hostility, although the majority of photographic evidence[19] of fairies is pretty clearly pareidolia.

When it comes to fairies this comes into play because a person who sees fairies in leaf patterns is usually a person who is primed to see fairies in nature because they are intentionally looking for fairies. This also occurs in still photos of things like flying bugs where the image is out of focus on the bug, or the insect is highlighted or backlit creating the impression of a glowing amorphous creature with wings and legs. Instead of being understood as a trick of perception these images are put forward as proof of fairies.

Another aspect of this that I think needs to be considered is the way that those who do believe in fairies are expected to also believe that these photos represent fairies caught on film. There's a kind of group-think that happens around this and which strongly rejects those who try to discuss other possible explanations. I find this unfortunate as any and all phenomena should always be open to discussion and explanation. I have said before that in any case of a fairy experience the first thing to be done is apply Occam's Razor and look for the simplest and most likely explanation – only when that has been ruled out should we consider supernatural explanations as valid. I say this as someone who has a profound belief in these beings and whose spirituality is based on a foundation of that belief.

In folklore and modern anecdotes seeing fairies isn't about spotting something that looks a bit like a person in the shapes of leaves but is usually about seeing something that is clearly defined, present, and often interactive. And as we discussed in Chapter 1, the idea of tiny fairies is relatively recent and doesn't represent the entirety of what fairies are, just as the idea of fairies being insect-like or made of nature is very modern and niche.

We have accounts of fairies in various sizes up to six feet tall and these beings are clearly seen by the witnesses' physical eyes. Folklore contains multiple methods to gain the sight of fairies if one doesn't have it naturally, and many stories warning of the results of offending them by violating their privacy. Seeing fairies is certainly a thing that does happen and still happens to humans, including ones who were not expecting to see or encounter them, but these sightings are very different from what we find in most cases of fairy photos.

I think a significant underlying factor going on with this entire subject is the desire by some to prove that fairies are real. And to be honest I find this problematic, and not just because of the folklore that says violating fairy privacy brings serious consequences.

We shouldn't need to prove that these beings exist in order to believe in them, but should trust our own experiences and the belief we may have from our lives or study of the subject. It is also worth noting – must be noted I think – that many anecdotal and folkloric accounts of fairies describe beings that are between 18 inches and 6 feet tall and are clearly humanoid[20] in appearance and can be (and are) interacted with and in some cases spoken to, which are vastly at odds with the tiny, fleeting, and often ambiguously shaped creatures captured on film.

I find that any time belief is linked to a need for indisputable physical, technological proof that will sway the hardest of sceptics, the person will always be disappointed. While it may be nice to have such evidence of fairies, or ghosts, or even gods, we shouldn't need it in order to have belief in these beings. In this I think we need to learn a lesson from the Cottingley Fairies hoax, where a series of faked fairy photographs in 1917 were initially taken as real and then later disproved, causing a crisis of faith for many people who had anchored their belief in fairies to this earthly proof of their existence. I want to be clear here that pareidolia isn't a bad thing, necessarily, nor is apophenia. When scrying using water, smoke, clouds, or fire – for example – we are basically using pareidolia to tap into a precognitive ability and interpreting the images we see to get messages or answers. Pareidolia can also be used to interpret omens or engage with psychic phenomena. Just because there is a psychological explanation behind the process doesn't invalidate the effectiveness of it. I might argue that seeing fairies works differently because we aren't talking about interpreting a random pattern to get a message but trying to perceive an otherwise invisible being; however, readers may decide differently.

In the end, those who truly want to see fairies in random photos will see them. It behooves us as a community, though, I think, to understand pareidolia and to work on weeding out evidence that doesn't pass the Occam's Razor test. Fairies are no less real because we aren't getting photos of them every five minutes, and if we toss out all the images that are obviously leaves and bugs what we have left will be evidence with some merit. Because while I will be the first to say 95% to 99% of the pictures I've seen have clear earthly or tech explanations the remaining 1 – 5% don't, and that is very, very interesting indeed.

Healthy Scepticism

Building off of that last section let's discuss the need for healthy scepticism. People who believe in fairies often enough seek to share that belief. We tell stories, both our own and ones passed down, and we find value in sharing our belief with others. Telling people to respect fairy places, to be careful not to damage fairy trees, speaking of the consequences of fairy friendship and fairy wrath.

Sometimes, though, that desire to share belief becomes a need to prove that these beings are real in a tangible physical way, and that far too often becomes problematic. We've already discussed one aspect of that above, and I'd like to look at some instances where the quest to try to prove what we believe is real has led to the exact opposite happening.

Over the years there have been several hoaxes relating to fairies, some intentional and some perhaps not. These are usually photos that circulate purporting to show fairies captured in natural settings. Unlike pareidolia, hoax photos are images where the fairy has been intentionally inserted into the image by the photographer and then the photo passed off as genuine. The most famous example, of course, is the Cottingley Fairy photos, a series of photographs taken by two young girls that showed them surrounded by or observing groups of winged fairies. Photography was a fairly new technology at the time and the images fooled many people, including author Sir Arthur Conan Doyle, who was a strong proponent of the girls and their fairies. The Cottingley fairies caused contention for decades until, in 1981, one of the girls, now an old woman, confessed the images were of paper cut-out fairies set up in the frame.

The controversy around the Cottingley hoax, as well as around similar hoaxes where people intentionally took pictures after situating a realistic fairy statue, doll, or other image within a natural setting, is nearly endless with some people. The harm caused by these hoaxes comes in with the way they erode actual belief and also give the impression that all fairy belief is rooted in such false premises.

A gaff is an object created to be misrepresented as something else; the term in this usage comes from circus sideshows which were well known for using fakes to deceive an audience into belief. Unlike hoaxes, gaffs provide a physical object that people can visit and see for themselves. The most famous example (and pertinent to our wider point here) from the 19ᵗʰ century sideshow era may be Barnum's 'Feejee Mermaid' which was the torso of a monkey sewn onto the body of a fish and presented as the corpse of a real mermaid.

Gaffs in the modern fairy community do exist and, I'd argue, cause more problems now than the old circus ones did. In 2007 the image of an alleged dead fairy, wings still attached, was supposedly discovered in Derbyshire and in 2017 the tiny skeletal remains of what was described as a pixie were supposedly found in North Carolina. Both were actually art pieces, the work of a man named Dan Baines who perpetuated the hoaxes. Despite the questionable nature of the remains and rather obvious art-piece quality of both photos still circulate all over social media and many people still believe they are genuine.

The desire to have solid evidence proving that fairies exist is, in my opinion, a product of our sceptical modern world that seeks to label, categorize, and define everything around us down to the smallest particle and teaches us that a thing isn't real unless it's scientifically understood. The reality is while certain things can be disproven (like the flat earth argument), when it comes to spiritual things and intangible beliefs physical proof is simply not the bedrock that we build from.

Is it possible that we may someday empirically prove fairies exist? Sure. Science is always finding new things, and even proving the existence of things that were thought to be myth or extinct. There was a time when gorillas were widely thought to be a myth outside areas they were found living in, for example, and there have been several cases of animals that were thought extinct being found alive years or decades later. We know a lot less about the world we live in than we like to think we do. But such objective proof shouldn't be necessary for spiritual belief, and I think we should always use critical thinking in these situations rather than throwing ourselves into believing things that are easily shown to be fakes.

The problem with this quest for proof, especially with a subject like fairies, is that it sets the stage for hoaxes and gaffs and for material to be put forward that is easily disproved, all of which harms the reputation of believers and the wider idea of belief in these things. Hoaxes are found out and uncovered, gaffs are shown to be art pieces, and when that happens the idea of believing in fairies becomes foolish and the territory of the gullible. In seeking proof, in desperately clinging to these fakes as proof, the exact opposite is accomplished and belief is eroded instead of upheld.

Ultimately when it comes to fairies belief is rooted in one of two things (if not both). People believe because they have had experiences of their own which cannot be explained otherwise, and people believe because they find truth in the stories of folklore and anecdotal accounts. I have believed in these beings since I was a child and there is nothing that would dissuade me from that belief – but I also understand that my belief isn't predicated on others agreeing with me or my being able to convince anyone else. The Fairy Faith isn't something that proselytizes or preaches the way that formal religions do; it's a belief system that's built on experience and voluntary participation.

Believing fully that fairies exist doesn't mean believing every single piece of evidence put forward as 'proof' of that existence. Discernment is important and doesn't – shouldn't – diminish belief especially in the 21st century when we are so easily surrounded by CGI fairy videos, photos, and hoaxes used to advertise artwork.

Chapter 7

Modern Fairies and Fiction

Because – as I hope I've shown at this point – it's almost impossible to separate modern fairy belief from the influence of modern fiction I'd like to end this book by taking a look at some of the ways that current fairy beliefs, especially in the US, have been shaped by fiction and the ways that fiction is being applied to practical belief. This subject is a complex one and leads into questions about the nature of fairies themselves – and also reflects the way that they have seemingly flowed along with human literature and understandings across the centuries. In other words, we can't understand fairies at any point in history without understanding the fiction written about them at that time as well and this is as true today as it was four hundred years ago.

I want to be clear at the beginning that pointing out that something is a more modern belief isn't a judgment on that belief. I happen to personally agree with some new beliefs, but I still think it's important to be clear about what is new and what is older. My goal here is simply to help differentiate between traditional folklore beliefs and modern beliefs rooted in fiction and popculture by teasing out some threads of modern belief that come from fiction.

Seasonal Fairy Courts – This is something that has grown out of urban fantasy across the last several decades, jumping off the older ideas of the Scottish Seelie and Unseelie courts[16] but removing any moral implications in the names and simply tying them to seasons. In some cases the terms summer and winter court are used interchangeably with Seelie and Unseelie while in others they stand alone, and the idea has been expanded into four seasonal courts each of which has a tone set by the season it belongs to.

Grey Court – like the seasonal courts this idea comes in from urban fantasy and paranormal romance and is used to represent a neutral group between the two Scottish fairy courts one of which is favourable to humans and one which is malicious. This group is also sometimes said to be formed by the more wild or solitary fairies. This is, of course, at odds with older folklore but is a system that seems to appeal to some modern fairy believers.

Who Rules The Courts? – so in folklore the Seelie and Unseelie are decidedly Scottish and unique to Scottish folklore, although the concept has taken root across the popular imagination. When we look at folkloric fairies and who is in charge, we find a wide array of local fairy kings and queens; however, in many corners of modern fairy belief folklore isn't the source being drawn on, rather people look to fiction. This means that Shakespeare's fairy Queens and King who have found a place in many modern novels have also found popularity in modern belief and are often named as the King and Queens of Fairy more generally or of the fairy courts specifically. There are therefore a wide array of answers to this question depending on which fiction author a person or group is looking to as a source. My own preference here, unsurprisingly, is to look to the older folklore but if you prefer the fiction route, I do suggest at least researching that named figure in the older folklore.

Nice Fairies – Fairies can be nice, but fairies are not nice by nature any more than people are. The idea that they all are all the time is entirely modern and an extreme break from actual folklore. I tend to point to the Victorians as the source on this one but it's hard to pinpoint exactly when and what started this shift and I think in reality it was probably a combination of the Victorian flower fairy obsession, the New Age movement's emphasis on the positive, and a conflation with the idea of spirit guides. This leaves us with modern popular culture fairies who don't resemble historic ones; certainly Disney's Tinkerbell is an example of the stereotypical modern fairy but H. M. Barrie's Tinkerbell was pretty vicious. Fairies in folklore were not to be messed with and could – and would – kill, maim, or hurt people for what may seem to us to be trifling slights. The current view of fairies as nice and helpful which can be found in belief based on fiction is drawing from this source and from authors who have tended to depict fairies as only helpful and nice beings.

Anthropomorphized fairies – I know I've emphasized repeatedly at this point the human like appearance of many fairies and I stand by that. However, the older understandings of fairies depict them as looking human but acting very inhumanly and often inhumanely. In contrast people drawing more on fiction as a source tend to perceive fairies as much like humans in thought and motivation, as the fairies of modern fiction are heavily anthropomorphised.

Fairies protecting the environment – Many modern pagans are firmly convinced that fairies are nature spirits and staunch protectors of the environment, an idea that appears in the works of pagan authors as well as movies (I'm looking at you Fern Gully). This is not something supported in actual folklore though but an idea that seems to have begun and gained popularity with humanity's own growing awareness of environmental concerns. It is true that many of the Fair Folk are extremely territorial and messing with their places is a profoundly bad idea – but this isn't due to a wider drive for them to protect our world so much as an urge for them to protect what belongs to them. There is, to my knowledge, not one single example in myth or folklore of the Good People appearing and warning anyone about the dangers of clear cutting forests, damning rivers, polluting, etc., prior to the modern era. And yes, those things did happen historically which is why Europe isn't covered in forest anymore and has lost a variety of native species to extinction due to hunting.

These are only a handful of examples of ways that modern fairylore differs from traditional fairylore and has been influenced by popculture. Indeed new fiction and new movies continue to come out and the popular ones seem to inevitably find a way to effect what people believe about the Other Crowd. For example, when a recent movie featuring a selkie came out (and a great movie it was too) which had the plot twist that the selkie couldn't speak without her sealskin coat I started seeing people repeating that tidbit as if it were traditional folklore, even though it is not. In a culture today where many people are disconnected from the traditional folklore and plugged into mass media and popculture it should not be surprising that it is fiction and movies that are shaping people's fairy beliefs rather than actual traditional folklore.

Recommendations for Fictional Fairies

Since I often talk about my concerns with modern fiction and its portrayal of fairies, particularly the way they end up being humanized, and have just listed several ways that fiction influences modern fairy belief I want to wrap things up with a list of books, shows, and movies I would recommend for people looking for good fairy-themed fiction.

These are the main books that I suggest people look for if they want good folkloric depictions of fairies in modern stories. No books is going to be 100% perfect but these are as close as I can think of, and they are also good stories.

Books

Lords and Ladies by Terry Pratchett – a book in Pratchett's Disc World series I chose Lords and Ladies specifically because his view of the elves here is pretty spot on for how inhuman and inhumane, they can be. To quote the book:

... people didn't seem to be able to remember what it was like with the elves around. Life was certainly more interesting then, but usually because it was shorter. And it was more colorful, if you liked the color of blood.

The Call by Peadar O'Guilin – a very well written alternate reality story set in a world where modern Ireland has been cut off from the rest of the world by fairy magic, and all humans are kidnapped as teenagers into Fairy. Most don't return alive. It's a wonderful depiction of fairies as monstrous and inhuman which is so often missing from other works.

The Dubh Linn series by Ruth Frances Long – a young adult series that blends folklore, folk belief, and modern Dublin into a cohesive fairy story.

Faery Sworn by Ron C Neito – a very creative story but overall fairly true to the folklore. Some variance on what the Seelie and Unseelie courts are called, but does a great job of including things like aversion to iron, viciousness, time slip between Fairy and Earth, and etiquette. My only critique would be at the idea that there are only single beings in some of the categories we know from folklore, ie 'the kelpie' 'the nucklevee', but that's a fairly minor quibble.

The Knowing by Kevan Manwaring – an excellent blend of older fairylore and the modern world. Based on the story of rev. Robert Kirk but imagining his descendants into our time, very accurate to older fairylore.

Good Fairies of New York by Martin Millar – a unique look at urban fairies, although I usually try to avoid stories of small winged fae this one is worth the read. I particularly liked the multicultural aspects the author brought into the city fairies.

Jonathan Strange and Mr. Norrell by Susanna Clark – complicated story about magicians in 19th century England but has a great deal of fairylore in it as well as accurate depictions of the Good People. I recommend both the book and the television series.

Spiritwalk by Charles de Lint – set in Canada, focused around a building, great mix of Celtic and North American fairylore.

Toby Daye series by Seanan McGuire – modern fairies in America, reasonably close to folklore in many respects especially as regards politics in Fairy.

The Elfhome series by Wen Spencer – really interesting and creative look at an alternate reality where science has created an interdimensional gate that has accidentally shifted modern Pittsburgh into elfhome. Mixes tech with magic in fun ways, and uses Japanese folklore as a base. However, it does take some creative liberties with that folklore that a Western audience may not fully recognize.

Series
Siren – On Freeform and Hulu, the series is in its third season. A rare show about mermaids that depicts them as dangerous predators of the sea, the series begins with one mermaid captured and used for government experiments and another wandering onto land to find her. The folklore here is a blend of some genuine material about mermaids (not the Disney sort) and some fantasy for plot purposes in the show. Despite this it has a strong feel to it and the storyline is, in my opinion, interesting. Definitely worth a try for people who like mermaid lore or the darker side of fairy stories.

Movies
The Secret of Kells –The Secret of Kells is a movie about a

young scribe in medieval Ireland who befriends a forest spirit named Aisling. Aisling is shown as somewhat childlike in her appearance but has powerful magic and shows up to help the main character when he is most in need of it.

Song of the Sea – by the same people who made Secret of Kells. Song of the Sea is the story of a young boy named Ben and his sister Saoirse. Their mother is a selkie and she left them to return to the sea the night Saoirse was born; Ben is human but his little sister is not and this forms in many ways the crux of the tension in the movie. It takes some liberties with Irish mythology but tells a great story and is full of fairies of different types all trying to get back to the Otherworld but trapped here. Only the song of a selkie can open the passage to Fairy, but the only selkie left on Earth is Saoirse and she's mute.

Seulseulhago Chalranhashin: Dokkaebi [English title 'Goblin: the lonely and great God'] – In fairness this is a Korean pop-drama so it is at points overly melodramatic and saccharine. However, that said it is also a fascinating look at the folklore around the dokkaebi, spirits who are roughly similar to the western concepts of fairies; the word dokkaebi is translated as goblin. This serial drama follows the story of one particular 'goblin' and his search for the person who can free him from his curse: the prophesied goblin's bride.

Labyrinth – A classic movie based on the lore of Changelings; a girl asks the goblins to take her little brother away and they do, forcing her to enter into a bargain with the Goblin King to try to win him back. Throughout the movie we see a huge range of fairies from dangerous to comical. Campy in places but has a lot of good material in it.

Pan's Labyrinth – Fabulous visual effects and a grim story, Pan's

Labyrinth weaves together modern myth and older folklore. I like this one in particular because it also explores the connection between the dead and fairies, something that doesn't often show up in movies (or books for that matter). The movie is full of many allusions to classic tropes from fairytales and mythology as well as a nod to the archetypal hero's journey.

The Hallow – one of my favourites on this list. Definitely leans into the genre of horror further than the folklore might merit and the actual depiction of the fairies is more zombie than fairy. But it draws on genuine tradition for the premise of the story, which centres on a couple who move to a small Irish town and ignore warnings to stay out of the forest which belongs to the 'hallow' aka fairies. Bonus points from me for being filmed entirely in Ireland.

Secret of Roan Inish – Another of my personal favourites, the story of a girl named Fiona who is sent to live with her grandparents and begins to unravel some family secrets which centre on the island the family left when Fiona was a small child, and the loss of her younger brother Jaimie. A story of selkies and the way that folklore can be interwoven through generations and affect people in the modern world.

So there you have it. This covers a range of genres and age groups, a variety of kinds of fairies and cultures, and I think offers some ideas for what can constitute good representations of fairies in modern fiction.

Conclusion

The world of Fairy is present still today just as the beings who inhabit it are and the way humans interact with and experience this world and these beings is more diverse than ever before. Human belief around fairies is shaped by fiction, which in turn shapes expectations and encounters, but in the same way these fairy beings seem to grow and evolve alongside human culture so that they change as we do. Is this all a reflection purely of human belief and expectations? Are fairies themselves shaped by human belief or do they appear to us intentionally, as we expect, through their own magic? Ultimately the answers to these question hinge entirely on your personal belief around the reality of fairies and how much personal power and agency you think they have – and I can't tell you what to think here. I can only do what I've already done by laying out what evidence we have and sharing my own thoughts and opinions so that you can draw your own conclusions.

Traditional fairy beliefs come to us across generations, reinforced by belief and practice. What makes these beliefs traditional is two main factors, I think: that they exist within a cultural framework and are passed down through successive generations, and that they represent genuine beliefs that people adhered to. Even today when we talk about beliefs in cultures like Iceland or Ireland, while contemporary people might deny that they themselves believe in the stories and folk practices they pass on, they do not question that their predecessors and other people do. It is these layers of past belief that build on each other and form the foundation of traditional belief. When a story is shared of someone experiencing being fairy-led or hearing a Bean Sidhe it is unquestioned that the person who had the experience genuinely believed it occurred and passed it on the same way they would have a story of seeing a rare bird or meeting a famous human.

For those seeking fairy beliefs today the sources are often confusing and convoluted. The traditional fairy beliefs are certainly still there and are easier to find than they ever have been, but the exact same thing that makes them more readily available to a wider audience are the same things that muddy the waters and add to the confusion. Fairy fiction is more popular than ever and far more detached from older beliefs; some storytellers take pride in overturning what they consider to be tropes by going against the older fairy beliefs while others take only the name of a being or concept and then reinvent it and yet others try to adhere as closely as they can to the folklore. It's no wonder that people are confused by this but we must also be aware of what a strong influence these sources are on 21st century fairies which don't and can't exist separate from the people who believe in them.

For people disconnected from the cultures who still actively have fairy beliefs, this mix of traditional beliefs and new creations can be confusing, especially when spirituality is added to the mix. People seeking fairies today, if they want to rely on the older beliefs, have to be cautious then to be aware of the pop-fiction and gaming pieces and to be clear about the sources they are pulling from. We can acknowledge fairies as a modern phenomenon and have experiences with them today while also being aware of the way our world and culture shapes our beliefs about them.

I began this book by saying that I'd be presenting a variety of ideas and opinions and that some of them might be contradictory or challenge a person's preconceived notions about fairies. I think that we've covered a lot of ground here in discussing how fairies have changed over time, how they relate to the 21st century, and how fiction impacts our belief and I know that in the midst of all that were many ideas that need to be further unpacked. I really hope that this book offers readers an opportunity to contemplate those ideas and to delved deeper into their own beliefs, as much as it has hopeful offered a basic guide these beings in the world today.

This is a beginning, not an ending.

Appendix A

Common Folklore Terms

I wanted to offer a quick and very rough guide to terms used around material connected to folklore and hence fairies. I find that this subject can be very confusing for people and hope this may help a bit with that, particularly for those who are planning to delve deeper into this subject. Disclaimer – these definitions are based in my own understanding of these concepts as an amateur folklorist.

Folklore – according to Oxford dictionary folklore is *"the traditional beliefs, customs, and stories of a community, passed through the generations by word of mouth"*. Folklore has several key aspects including both its oral nature as well as its existence within a community. Folklore is also fluid and evolving, showing change in line with the community it is attached to.

Michael Fortune's YouTube videos of people being interviewed and discussing their community's or their family's fairy beliefs is an example of folklore.

Folkloresque – Also sometimes called folklorism, folkloresque is material that is rooted in folklore concepts of motifs but which heavily incorporates creativity and fiction to create something new. The folkloresque isn't properly folklore – it isn't representative of a group's beliefs or practices – but is inspired by or based on existing folklore. Another key difference between folklore and the folkloresque is that the folkloresque exists in a fixed form.

The movie 'Labyrinth' can be described as folkloresque.

Anecdote – an anecdote is a personal story being recounted by the person who experienced it or passed on as such. It represents a real person describing events they witnessed or experienced. Someone describing their own encounter with a fairy is an anecdotal account.

Retellings – Much of the Victorian material we have, as well as some popular modern material, falls into this category. Retellings represent folklore that is being preserved in written form with additions from the author; there can often be a fine line between a retelling and the folkloresque but while retellings often add flourishes and drama they generally adhere to the broad strokes of the original folklore. Lady Wilde's work may best be described as retellings.

Fiction – is written work that describes imaginary stories or relates events that aren't true. This is why works of fiction usually include disclaimers that the work was created by the author and any resemblance to real people or places, etc., is unintentional. Fiction is an exercise in human imagination and is usually predicated on telling an interesting story. 'The Dresden Files' is an example of fiction.

There is often debate on whether or not folklore is fiction, but in my opinion, this presupposes that folklore is untrue and was created at some point purely for entertainment, which ignores the key aspect of folklore as belief and practice of a community. Whether or not stories of selkie wives did happen, they represent active belief in a community, with attached practices, and were understood as true by the people who believed in them. Fiction in contrast is created intentionally to be a story for entertainment. This is an essential and pivotal difference.

Bibliography

Acland, A., (2017) Tam Lin Balladry

Atsma, A., (2017) Satyroi http://www.theoi.com/Georgikos/ Satyroi.html

Bovey, A., (2006) Monsters and Grotesques in Medieval Manuscripts

Briggs, K., (1976) A Dictionary of Fairies

Cutchin, J., (2015) A Trojan Feast

--- (2018) Thieves in the Night

Duchas (2020) Duchas.ie; Fairies Retrieved from https://www. duchas.ie/en/src?q=fairies

Dunkerson, C., (2017) Do the Elves in Tolkien's Stories Have Pointed Ears? http://tolkien.slimy.com/essays/Ears.html

Evans-Wentz, W., (1911) Fairy Faith in Celtic Countries

Fairy Folklore (2020) Sussex Archaeology and Folklore

Grose, F., (1811) Dictionary of the Vulgar Tongue

Gundarsson, K., (2007). Elves, Wights, and Trolls

Hall, A., (2007) Elves in Anglo-Saxon England

Jackson, W., (2017) What Are the Unicorns and Satyrs in the Bible?

Kirk, R., (1691) The Secret Commonwealth of Elves, Fauns, and Fairies

KJV (2017) Official King James Bible online https://www. kingjamesbibleonline.org/

Kruse, J., (2019) "Ray of Light" Tinkerbell and Luminous Fairies', retrieved from https://britishfairies.wordpress. com/2019/01/06/ray-of-light-tinkerbell-and-luminous-fairies/

Lang, A., and Kirk, R., (1893) The Secret Commonwealth of Elves, Fauns, and Fairies

Martineau, J., (1997) Victorian Fairy Painting

Mikl, A., (2004) Fairy Paintings in 19th Century Art and Late 20th Century Art: A Comparative Study http://www2.uwstout.

edu/content/lib/thesis/2004/2004mikla.pdf

Narvaez, P., (1991) The Good People: New Fairylore Essays

Purkiss, D., (2000) At the Bottom of the Garden: A Dark History of Fairies, Hobgoblins, and Other Troublesome Things

Rodriguez, A., (2017) Old Testament Demonology

Shakespeare, W., (1980) Romeo and Juliet. Retrieved from http://shakespeare.mit.edu/romeo_juliet/full.html

Sikes, W., (1880) British Goblins: Welsh folklore, Fairy mythology, Legends, and Traditions

Silver, C., (1999) Strange & Secret Peoples: Fairies and the Victorian Consciousness

Vallee, J., (1969) Passport to Magonia

Wilby, E., (2009) Cunningfolk and Familiar Spirits

Wilde, E., (1888) Irish Cures, Mystic Charms, & Superstitions

Wimberly, L., (1965) Folklore in the English & Scottish Ballads

Wirt, S., (1880) British Goblins

Wright, A., (2009) Puck Through the Ages https://www.boldoutlaw.com/puckrobin/puckages.html

Yeats, W., (1902) Celtic Twilight

Young, S., (2018) Fairy Census

Endnotes

1. Glamour is a type of magic that fools the senses, particularly sight causing humans to see things very differently than they actually are.
2. Which is what sceptics and nonbelievers would say anyway, so this can all get very circular very quickly.
3. Urban fantasy is a fiction genre which depicts magical creatures, including fairies, within the modern human world, often existing in secret alongside human society.
4. Although in fairness Carnival Row is more of an alternate reality Steampunk fantasy than urban fantasy it does still forward a more integrated view of fairies.
5. The text is sometimes given 'as 'half an 'nch' but Briggs rightly suggests this is a scribal error as that size is incompatible with the actions described – such as carrying a young frog – within the text. Despite this the error has undoubtedly influenced later perceptions of the size of fairies.
6. A version of this section also appears in my book A New Dictionary of Fairies.
7. I'm focusing specifically here on Western culture and European folklore because I am not well versed enough in other areas of folklore to speak to the ear-shapes of fairies throughout the world. Although that would be an interesting topic to discuss the research involved is beyond the scope of this blog at this time. I would tentatively suggest based on what I know of specifically Japanese and Chinese folklore as well as Native American folklore tha' it's likely most fairies have round ears as when in a human-like form they are generally described as being able to pass as human or otherwise looking human, however, I cannot say so with certainty without a great deal more research.
8. For example, Isaiah 34: 4: "The wild beasts of the desert

shall also meet with the wild beasts of the island, and the satyr shall cry to his fellow; the screech owl also shall rest there, and find for herself a place of rest." – KJV Bible

9. In fairness he did seem to later pull back from this description and it's an open ended debate as to whether his ultimate intention was for his elves to have pointed ears or not.

10. RPG = role playing game.

11. See Fairy Census entry #22 for one example.

12. There is, of course, no way to know how long they have existed in oral cultures.

13. Of course, there are some exceptions, but again we can find places in our own world that reflect various historical time periods as well.

14. Let us all take a moment to appreciate the idea of one of the Gentry appearing today in bell bottoms and tie dye, or a poodle skirt.

15. This is from a story where a servant girl fails to leave out fresh water overnight for the Good Folk to cook with so they prick her and use her blood to make their bread instead, causing her to fall ill. Her health is restored only when she finds out what has happened and manages to get a piece of the bread for herself to eat.

16. To be clear as I move forward with my discussion on this point, I am autistic and I am aware that people in the community embrace the term. This outlines why I do not do so. I am not telling anyone how to self-identify, only discussing the actual history of the term and its application to people. If you personally choose to identify as a changeling that is your choice, however, I am deeply uncomfortable with the label being applied externally to children.

17. Modern French for fairy is fée.

18. Obviously, given this is my 10th book on or related to the

subject and I've been publicly teaching about it since 2000.

19. There are also issues with gaffs, or basically artwork passed off as genuine fairies or fairy bodies. We'll discuss those presently.

20. Of course, some encounters are with fairy beings in animal forms as well.

21. The Seelie and Unseelie Courts themselves and the entire idea of two courts as such is itself probably comparatively newer as well only really coming in within the last 200 years or so.

MOON
BOOKS

PAGANISM & SHAMANISM

What is Paganism? A religion, a spirituality, an alternative belief system, nature worship? You can find support for all these definitions (and many more) in dictionaries, encyclopaedias, and text books of religion, but subscribe to any one and the truth will evade you. Above all Paganism is a creative pursuit, an encounter with reality, an exploration of meaning and an expression of the soul. Druids, Heathens, Wiccans and others, all contribute their insights and literary riches to the Pagan tradition. Moon Books invites you to begin or to deepen your own encounter, right here, right now.

If you have enjoyed this book, why not tell other readers by posting a review on your preferred book site.

Recent bestsellers from Moon Books are:

Journey to the Dark Goddess
How to Return to Your Soul
Jane Meredith
Discover the powerful secrets of the Dark Goddess and
transform your depression, grief and pain into healing
and integration.
Paperback: 978-1-84694-677-6 ebook: 978-1-78099-223-5

Shamanic Reiki
Expanded Ways of Working with Universal Life Force Energy
Llyn Roberts, Robert Levy
Shamanism and Reiki are each powerful ways of healing; together,
their power multiplies. *Shamanic Reiki* introduces techniques to
help healers and Reiki practitioners tap ancient healing wisdom.
Paperback: 978-1-84694-037-8 ebook: 978-1-84694-650-9

Pagan Portals – The Awen Alone
Walking the Path of the Solitary Druid
Joanna van der Hoeven
An introductory guide for the solitary Druid, *The Awen Alone* will
accompany you as you explore, and seek out your own place
within the natural world.
Paperback: 978-1-78279-547-6 ebook: 978-1-78279-546-9

A Kitchen Witch's World of Magical Herbs & Plants
Rachel Patterson
A journey into the magical world of herbs and plants, filled with
magical uses, folklore, history and practical magic. By popular
writer, blogger and kitchen witch, Tansy Firedragon.
Paperback: 978-1-78279-621-3 ebook: 978-1-78279-620-6

Medicine for the Soul
The Complete Book of Shamanic Healing
Ross Heaven
All you will ever need to know about shamanic healing and how to
become your own shaman...
Paperback: 978-1-78099-419-2 ebook: 978-1-78099-420-8

Shaman Pathways – The Druid Shaman
Exploring the Celtic Otherworld
Danu Forest
A practical guide to Celtic shamanism with exercises and
techniques as well as traditional lore for exploring the Celtic
Otherworld.
Paperback: 978-1-78099-615-8 ebook: 978-1-78099-616-5

Traditional Witchcraft for the Woods and Forests
A Witch's Guide to the Woodland with Guided Meditations and
Pathworking
Mélusine Draco
A Witch's guide to walking alone in the woods, with guided
meditations and pathworking.
Paperback: 978-1-84694-803-9 ebook: 978-1-84694-804-6

Wild Earth, Wild Soul
A Manual for an Ecstatic Culture
Bill Pfeiffer
Imagine a nature-based culture so alive and so connected,
spreading like wildfire. This book is the first flame...
Paperback: 978-1-78099-187-0 ebook: 978-1-78099-188-7

Naming the Goddess
Trevor Greenfield
Naming the Goddess is written by over eighty adherents and
scholars of Goddess and Goddess Spirituality.
Paperback: 978-1-78279-476-9 ebook: 978-1-78279-475-2

Shapeshifting into Higher Consciousness
Heal and Transform Yourself and Our World with Ancient
Shamanic and Modern Methods
Llyn Roberts
Ancient and modern methods that you can use every day to
transform yourself and make a positive difference in the world.
Paperback: 978-1-84694-843-5 ebook: 978-1-84694-844-2

Readers of ebooks can buy or view any of these bestsellers by
clicking on the live link in the title. Most titles are published in
paperback and as an ebook. Paperbacks are available in traditional
bookshops. Both print and ebook formats are available online.

Find more titles and sign up to our readers' newsletter at
http://www.johnhuntpublishing.com/paganism
Follow us on Facebook at https://www.facebook.com/MoonBooks
and Twitter at https://twitter.com/MoonBooksJHP